BIRMINGHAM UNIVERSITY LIBRARY

THIS BOOK MUST BE RETURNED
IMMEDIATELY IF RECALLED FOR
THE USE OF ANOTHER BORROWER,
OTHERWISE ON OR BEFORE THE
LATEST DATE BELOW

NEW BOOK

THIS BOOK IS NOT AVAILABLE
FOR LOAN UNTIL

D1615239

AN INTRODUCTION TO NATIONAL ACCOUNTS STATISTICS

471871 11/9/8

By the same author

BASIC MATHEMATICS
INDEX NUMBERS IN THEORY AND PRACTICE
MACRO-ECONOMIC THEORY
MATHEMATICAL ANALYSIS FOR ECONOMISTS
MATHEMATICAL ECONOMICS

AN INTRODUCTION TO NATIONAL ACCOUNTS STATISTICS

R. G. D. Allen

© R. G. D. Allen 1980

All rights reserved. No part of this publication may be
reproduced or transmitted, in any form or by any means,
without permission

First published 1980 by
THE MACMILLAN PRESS LTD
London and Basingstoke
Companies and representatives
throughout the world

Printed in Great Britain by
Billing and Sons Ltd
Guildford, London, Oxford Worcester

British Library Cataloguing in Publication Data

Allen, *Sir* Roy George Douglas
  An introduction to national accounts statistics
  1. National income – Accounting
  2. Macroeconomics – Statistical methods
  339.3   HB601

  ISBN 0–333–28195–0 (hardcover)
  ISBN 0–333–30438–1 (paperback)

1228402

HB 601

A

The paperback edition of this book is sold subject to the
condition that it shall not, by way of trade or otherwise, be lent,
resold, hired out, or otherwise circulated without the publisher's
prior consent, in any form of binding or cover other than that
in which it is published and without a similar condition including
this condition being imposed on the subsequent purchaser

Contents

Acknowledgement

The author and publishers wish to thank the Controller of Her Majesty's Stationery Office for permission to include the tables and statistics from government publications.

1 The National Accounts

1.1 Outline of Text

The first four chapters that follow deal with the money flows of the national accounts, valued at current prices. The emphasis is on the concepts, on methods of estimating the main aggregates and on ways of setting out the sector accounts. Later chapters take up the problem of valuing aggregates in real terms at constant prices and the price index numbers implied by these real measures. There are numerous illustrations throughout, in the form of tabulations taken from official publications.

The text is an 'introduction' in two senses. First, it makes no attempt at full coverage of the very extensive and extremely detailed national accounts. It deals at some length with the main aggregates, and with their division into broad components, as set out in the summary tables of the national accounts. It says something about the accounts of the main sectors: personal and corporate sectors, central and local government, international transactions in the balance of payments. It goes on to explain what is meant by the summary capital account, and by the complete balance of payments on current and capital account. But no more: there is nothing on sector capital accounts, on stocks of fixed capital or on transactions in financial assets.

Second, even when a subject is treated fairly fully, the text avoids going into fine detail, except where it provides striking illustrations of, or insights into, the methodology of the national accounts. The amount of detail built up in the accounts over years of development is enormous. It is to be seen in the sheer bulk of the official handbook:

Central Statistical Office, *National Accounts Statistics: Sources and Methods*, edited by Rita Maurice (London: HMSO, 1968).

Instead of going into detail each time, at several stages the text gives page references to this publication, which is referred to simply as *Sources and Methods*.

/It is not enough to illustrate with figures for one particular year. It is
/equally – indeed more – important to show changes in the aggregates
/ and their components from one year to another. /To illustrate the
methodology in the early chapters of the text, estimates for 1978 are
compared with corresponding figures for 1975. So changes are shown
over the interesting three-year period from 1975 to 1978, years of slow
recovery from the bottom of a depression. When changes in real
national income and in prices are identified and examined later in the
text, a closer look can be taken at economic developments with the aid of
figures over a complete cycle from the peak in 1973, through the trough
in 1975 and on through the subsequent recovery.

1.2 Terminology and References

There are various terms in use for the concepts of the national accounts.
There has been, and still is, a fairly widespread preference for the
adjective 'social' rather than 'national'. Sir John Hicks in his book *The
Social Framework*, 4th edn (Oxford: OUP, 1971) writes of the social
income and the social product within a set of social accounts. When it is
a matter of calculation or estimation, however, he usually refers to the
national income. Dr Stuvel elects to use social rather than national in G.
Stuvel, *Systems of Social Accounts* (Oxford: OUP, 1965). On the other
hand, official statistics in this country have used 'national income and
expenditure' in their titles since the beginning in the 1940s and the
government handbook refers to the 'national accounts'. This is in line
with the international practice which has grown up around the following
publications:

> United Nations, *A System of National Accounts*, Studies in Methods,
> series F, no. 2 (revision 3), (New York: United Nations, 1968); and
> OECD, *A Standardised System of National Accounts* (Paris: OECD,
> 1959).

There is some tendency, in this country at least, to try to get the benefits
of both worlds by referring to the national income within the social
accounts. Sir Richard Stone illustrates this in J. R. N. and Giovanna
Stone, *National Income and Expenditure* 10th edn, (London: Bowes &
Bowes, 1977) and *Social Accounting and Economic Models* (Bowes &
Bowes, 1959). The same is true of the well-known text: H. C. Edey, A. T.
Peacock and R. A. Cooper, *National Income and Social Accounting*, 3rd
edn (London: Hutchinson, 1967).

The present text, following standard international practice, uses the term 'national accounts' throughout. Indeed the main distinction made is not between the national and social accounts, but something quite different: the term 'national' as used in national income or product is intended to refer to income of UK nationals whether derived at home or abroad; in contrast, 'domestic' in the terms domestic income or product refers to what is produced in the UK domestic economy, the consequent income being paid either to UK nationals or to foreigners.

Broad references are made in the text, rather loosely, to the national income and the national accounts. But for the most part, and certainly when precision is required, a careful distinction is made between those aggregates at the 'national' level and those which are 'domestic'.

1.3 Publications

The national accounts statistics of this country are calculated and published quarterly and annually. Annual statistics are given in great detail, those for quarters rather less so. Apart from brief references to quarterly data, the present text is developed entirely in terms of annual figures. There is therefore no need to refer to a 'period', meaning a quarter or a year, as the case may be; the exposition relates simply to 'years' throughout. In describing index numbers, for example, such convenient shorthand as 'expenditure in the current year at constant (base year) prices' can be used. It is always to be remembered, however, that the official statistics include quarterly as well as annual series.

Annual statistics are issued each September in a publication referred to throughout the text by its short and commonly used title, the *Blue Book*; namely:

Central Statistical Office, *National Income and Expenditure* (London: HMSO).

Unless otherwise stated, the volume referred to throughout is that for 1979, which contains full details up to the end of 1978. Quarterly statistics are published in *Economic Trends* under the title 'National Income and Expenditure' in January, April, July and October of each year. The April issue has figures up to and including the fourth quarter of the previous year so that the article appearing in April 1979 has the first (provisional) figures for the year 1978. The October issue, the first following the *Blue Book*, has longer runs of quarterly series than the other issues, all geared to the firm estimates of the *Blue Book*.

The *Blue Book* contains only one table on the overseas sector, a summary tabulation of international transactions derived from the current account of the UK balance of payments. The main source of data on the balance of payments, on capital as well as on current account, is therefore the annual *Pink Book*:

Central Statistical Office, *United Kingdom Balance of Payments* (London: HMSO).

published in August each year. Quarterly statistics appear in *Economic Trends* under the title United Kingdom Balance of Payments in March, June, September and December of each year. Since it comes out one month later, the *Blue Book* has figures on international transactions which are consistent with those of the immediately preceding *Pink Book*. Similarly, quarterly data on the national income are always consistent with those on the balance of payments in *Economic Trends* one month earlier.

Timeliness is an important matter in the production programme of such much-used statistics as those of the national accounts. The first adequately detailed figures on the national income for any given year appear in *Economic Trends* for the following April (generally available early in May). Some of the detail is published a month or so earlier, for instance information on consumers' expenditure as well as on the balance of payments. In addition, from late February onwards, the Central Statistical Office issues Press Notices containing statistical tables which are well in advance of their publication in *Economic Trends* and elsewhere.

2 Main Aggregates: Methods

2.1 Circular Flow of Income

The national income of the UK is the sum of money incomes received by UK nationals from current economic activity. It is a *money flow* in a specified time, here taken as a year. It is related to two other concepts, each a set of *current goods and services* valued at the ruling prices during the year. One set of goods and services consists of the output of UK nationals as producers. The other is the set of purchases made by UK nationals. Each includes capital goods and services as well as those for consumption. In a closed economy the absence of external trade ensures that the two sets are identical: what is produced by nationals is also purchased by them. They are of different composition in any actual economy. Some of the output of nationals consists of exports sold abroad; some of the purchases of nationals are goods and services imported from abroad.

Economists have developed the idea of income as flowing in a closed circuit and represented on a schematic diagram; see R. G. Lipsey and P. O. Steiner, *Economics*, 3rd edn (1972), Figs 26.1–26.6. In adopting this approach we can start with the simplifying assumptions that there is no external trade and no government. Figs 2.1 and 2.2 are drawn on these assumptions. They are relaxed when we allow, first, for external trade (in 2.2 below) and then for a government sector (in 2.3 below).

The simpler diagram of Fig. 2.1A has two sectors and two markets. The production sector is where the first set of goods and services originates: the output of nationals. The household sector is concerned with the second set of goods and services: the purchases of nationals. Money flows clockwise around the diagram, between the sectors and through the markets for factors and for products. Two views can be taken of the money flow.

From the point of view of the production sector, the aggregate value of output is the central variable; label it X. Attention is then directed to the first set of goods and services, as produced by nationals with a total value X at current prices. Money flows out of the production sector to

5

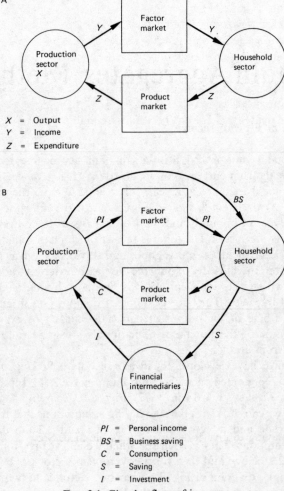

FIG. 2.1 Circular flow of income

the nationals whose services are hired on the factor market. The income so generated can be given the label Y: the sum of all incomes of the factors of production. To finance production, money flows into the production sector from the sale of the output on the product market. The expenditure on the goods and services in the product market can be denoted by Z, interpreted here as what emerges from the interaction of buyers and sellers on the market.

The same variables are viewed in a different light by the household sector. The money income Y flowing in is for services rendered to production. Households plan their expenditures, on the second set of goods and services, purchased out of income. The interaction between buyers and sellers on the product market again results in aggregate expenditure Z, which then flows into the production sector to finance output X.

In economic dynamics, there are time lags and the plans of producers and of households are not geared to one another in any given period. The three aggregates are not necessarily equal:

Output $X \neq$ income $Y \neq$ expenditure Z

X relates to the first set of goods and services, the output of the production sector. Y is the flow of income generated, passing from the production to the household sector. Z then relates to the second set of goods and services, the purchases made on the product market. But Z is also the flow of money into the production sector and available for financing X, completing the circular flow.

The inequalities are usefully examined from the angle of saving and investment. For this, the schematic diagram needs an additional sector, for financial intermediaries, as shown in Fig. 2.1B. The economic dynamics can be simplified, without much loss, by assuming no lag between output X and income Y and by taking consumption plans of households as realised. Then X equals Y, which in its turn is the sum of income paid out through the factor market (personal income) and undistributed profits which by-pass the market (business saving). Households split personal income into consumption and saving. Consumption C is realised as planned. Saving of households is added to business saving to give total saving S as planned. So:

$X = Y =$ personal income *plus* business saving $=$ consumption *plus* saving S

C is the constituent of Z which passes through the product market back to the production sector. Planned saving S gives rise to planned investment I through financial intermediaries and I is the other constituent of Z. On the present assumptions the economic–dynamic inequalities arise only because of a lack of synchronisation between saving and investment plans:

Ex ante: $X = Y = C + S$ and $Z = C + I$ where $S \neq I$

These relations form part of the familiar Keynesian system.

In the event and as a simple matter of book-keeping, output X, income Y and expenditure Z are identical totals. For each money deal involving (e.g.) output and income, the same money amount is assigned two ways, one to X and one to Y. The wage-bill in coalmining, for example, is allocated to X as part of value added in the coalmining industry and equally to Y as the employment income generated. All monies arising in current economic activity by nationals are accounted for; nothing is left floating loose. So:

Ex post: $X \equiv Y \equiv Z$ giving $C + S \equiv C + I$ and $S \equiv I$

Such book-keeping makes economic sense. As plans are translated into outcomes, households find that saving may not be realised as planned; there can be unintended saving (or dis-saving). Equally, financial intermediaries find that planned investment may not be achieved; there can be unintended investment (or dis-investment), e.g. in the form of build up (or running down) of stocks. Saving and investment are equal *ex post* with unplanned elements: unintended saving and/or unintended investment.

So it is with the national accounts of a closed economy. They pick up the aggregates X, Y and Z, identical *ex post*, and give them the labels 'national output', 'national income' and 'national expenditure'. It is the *totals X, Y* and *Z* which are identical by definition. The *components* of each are quite different, as indicated broadly in the boxes of Fig. 2.2.

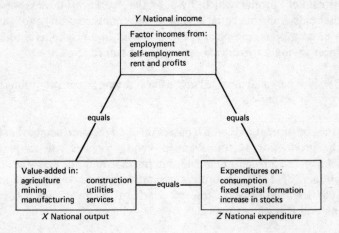

FIG. 2.2 National income, output and expenditure (closed economy)

The components of income are practical versions of rent, employment income and profits from the economists' land (and buildings), labour and capital – with self-employment income a mixture and with profits a reward for enterprise as well as a return on capital. The output box could be arranged to comprise the final goods and services, for consumption or for capital formation, valued at the end of the production line, or alternatively the contributions to output made by the various industries. In the second form, adopted in Fig. 2.2, each industry contributes its value added: sales and closing value of stocks *less* purchases and opening value of stocks. The expenditure box has components arranged on the consumption and capital formation division; they are purchases out of income and expenditures on output of final goods and services.

The national accounts show in detail how the components make up one and the same total and how they change over time. But they do not do more than this. They say nothing about economic dynamics, for example whether there is excess demand or a shortfall in saving and, if so, what the consequences are on such variables as inflation and employment.

Before we turn to methods of statistical estimation, we need to drop the simplifying assumptions. Fig. 2.1 could be modified to allow for external trade and for government, but only by becoming so complex as to defeat its purpose. It is better to be opportunist and to introduce, first, external trade and, then, government with statistical needs in mind. One matter requires particularly careful handling. When there is external trade, the two sets of goods and services aggregated in the national accounts are different: those which are produced for sale at home or abroad, with imports eliminated; and those purchased out of income, including their import content. The double role remains: expenditure on output and expenditure out of income.

2.2 National Accounts: Concepts and Labels

It is now assumed that there is external trade, but still no government. This enables the specification of the main concepts of the national accounts while leaving for later treatment the relatively minor complications arising from a government sector. It means that the aggregates summarised in Fig. 2.3 are simply at current prices. The distinction between factor cost and market prices is only needed later when there is a government levying indirect taxes and handing out subsidies.

Output	Income	Expenditure
Value added (gross) in domestic industries producing goods and services for consumption and investment	Factor income (gross) from employment, self-employment, rent and profits in the domestic economy	Consumers' expenditure by UK nationals and gross domestic investment
		Total domestic expenditure
Gross domestic output *plus* net property income from abroad	Gross domestic income *plus* net property income from abroad	(see text)
Gross national output ≡ Gross national income ≡ Gross national expenditure		

FIG. 2.3 Relations between output, income and expenditure

One distinction made in the national accounts is best introduced at once: that between gross and net valuations. Output, income and expenditure can be valued *gross* before provision for depreciation of capital assets, or *net* after such provision. Net values are to be obtained from gross by deduction of *capital consumption* as a measure of depreciation. The official national accounts of the UK concentrate almost exclusively on gross valuations, if only because estimates of capital consumption are very approximate. All the aggregates of Fig. 2.3 are gross values.

A more important distinction, and one essential to the appreciation of the national accounts, is that between aggregates at the *national* and those at the *domestic* levels. The nature of this distinction is best seen in terms of income.

Gross domestic income is the sum of all money incomes, before depreciation, arising from the current economic activity of all those, whether nationals or foreigners, concerned with the domestic economy of the UK. These incomes are shown in the middle column of Fig. 2.3, as in the income box of Fig. 2.2, as arising from employment, self-employment, rent and profits, all valued gross. The domestic economy comprises the group of all persons, non-profitmaking bodies and business enterprises operating within a production boundary enclosing the production sector shown schematically in Fig. 2.1.

The *production boundary* in its turn can be described, if not strictly defined, by listing what is in and what is out. This will be done as we proceed to introduce the various components of the national accounts; it is enough here to give an illustration. All UK companies, public and private, and all self-employed traders, partnerships and unincorporated businesses are in, as far as their operations in the UK are concerned. Their branches and subsidiaries overseas are out. All branches and subsidiaries operated in the UK by foreign concerns are in. The operators of UK-registered ships and aircraft are in, and so are the oil rigs in the UK part of the North Sea continental shelf. The production boundary is no rigid geographical one. It is, rather, a net sufficiently flexible to sweep in the British fishing fleet wherever it may be operating and the aircraft of British airlines wherever they may land and take off. There is, for example, something added to gross domestic income whenever a British vessel lands fish – home sales if at a port in the UK, exports if landed abroad.

On the other hand, *gross national income* is the sum of all money incomes accruing to UK nationals from their current economic activity. UK nationals are those persons – and by a convenient convention those non-profitmaking bodies and unincorporated enterprises – who reside for tax purposes in the UK. Their economic activity may be at home, within the domestic economy as circumscribed by the production boundary. Or it may be abroad through the operation of businesses or the ownership of property overseas. The incomes are not all actually received by nationals; some are to be attributed to them though handled on their behalf (e.g.) as undistributed profits by companies.

The difference between gross domestic and national income involves external transactions. We need to bring in the balance of international payments on current account, as published in detail in the annual *Pink Book* and in summary in the table on international transactions in the *Blue Book*. The balance is struck between credit items for inflows of funds into the UK and the corresponding debit items for outflows. One of the groups of items on each side is property income as the sum of interest, profits and dividends. The credit entry is property income received by UK nationals from abroad after deduction of any foreign taxes levied; the debit item is property income paid out of domestic income to foreigners after deduction of UK taxes. *Net property income from abroad* is the balance of credits over debits and it may be positive (net credit) or negative (net debit). In the balance of payments of the UK it is usually positive, net receipts from abroad.

Another group of items on each side of the balance of payments consists of current transfers from and to abroad. Examples are grants in aid, gifts, legacies and remittances from migrants. Some may be of a capital nature but for practical convenience all are counted as current. In the UK balance of payments current transfers to abroad almost inevitably exceed those from abroad. It is appropriate therefore to take *net transfers to abroad* as the balance, positive for the UK, of debits over credits.

In the national accounts, property income from or to abroad appears among items of income to be taken into account, whereas transfers from or to abroad are excluded with other transfers (2.7 below) from the main aggregates. Such transfers still need to be considered, as is made clear later, when looking at the way in which incomes are spent.

Gross domestic income arises within the domestic economy; it includes property incomes paid to foreigners in addition to incomes derived by UK nationals from domestic activity. Gross national income arises from all economic activity by UK nationals; some comes from domestic sources and the rest as property income from abroad. So one is got from the other: first remove property income paid to foreigners from gross domestic income and then add property income received from abroad by UK nationals to complete their total income from home and abroad:

> Gross national income = gross domestic income *plus*
> net property income from abroad   (A)

This completes the income column in the scheme of Fig. 2.3.

The parallel concepts of gross output at the two levels are shown in the first column of Fig. 2.3. *Gross domestic output* is the sum of values added by the industries making up the domestic economy, as in the output box of Fig. 2.2. By definition the value added of each industry is what is due as income to the factors of production so that

> Gross domestic output = gross domestic income   (B)

The identity (B) applies to the aggregates in *total* and it is represented by a line drawn across the first two columns of Fig. 2.3. The *components* of the two totals of (B) are different, as shown above the line of Fig. 2.3.

A rather conventional extension gives *gross national output*. Part of the income side of (B) is property income paid to foreigners – identify this as the part of the output side attributable to foreigners. Then add to the income side of (B) the property income received by UK nationals from abroad – identify this as the addition needed on the output side to represent the production activity of UK nationals abroad. So on the output side:

> Gross national output = gross domestic output *plus*
> net property income from abroad   (C)

which introduces in effect the concept of aggregate output of UK nationals at home and abroad. From (A), (B) and (C):

Gross national output = gross national income   (D)

an identity matching (B) and completing the output column of Fig. 2.3.

In view of (A) to (D), and the first two columns of Fig. 2.3, there is no need to distinguish between output and income as total aggregates at the domestic or at the national level. A single label is appropriate and one is in general use, *product*, for output and income alike. A reduction to symbols is also generally used:

GDP for *gross domestic product*; GNP for *gross national product*

Here GDP as output or income expresses the identity (B) and similarly GNP as the identity (D). GDP and GNP are neutral terms in the sense that it remains to specify whether their components are outputs or incomes.

Two concepts have now emerged. One is GDP for output or income in the domestic economy as circumscribed by the production boundary; the other is GNP for what UK nationals produce or get as income from their current economic activity at home and abroad.

As a technical point, note that GDP and GNP have arisen here from rather loose descriptions of 'production boundary' and of "UK nationals'. The official national accounts give stricter definitions in terms of a single concept of UK residents. The 1978 *Blue Book* (p. 107) puts the definitions briefly and in terms of prices specified as factor costs:

> *Gross national product at factor cost.* The total income of residents of the United Kingdom, before providing for depreciation or capital consumption. It is equal to the value at factor cost of the goods and services produced by United Kingdom residents *plus* their income from economic activity abroad and from property held abroad *less* the corresponding income in the United Kingdom of non-residents.
> *Gross domestic product at factor cost.* The total value at factor cost of the goods and services produced by United Kingdom residents before providing for depreciation or capital consumption.

The difficulty is that the term 'residents' is technically complicated – much more so than its popular usage would suggest. It takes nearly three pages of *Sources and Methods* to develop.

It seems better here to dodge the difficulty and to stick to the descriptive terms 'production boundary' and 'UK nationals'. They convey quite well the distinction between GDP at the domestic level and GNP at the national level.

The expenditure column remains to be added to Fig. 2.3. It is here that the two sets of goods and services – those produced and those purchased – are to be distinguished in developing the double role of expenditure.

Total domestic expenditure is the basic aggregate: the sum of all expenditures by UK nationals as consumers and of all gross investment in fixed assets and stocks within the domestic economy. This concept is not at the domestic level of gross domestic income, nor is it at the national level of gross national income. For this reason a separate line is drawn across the third column of Fig. 2.3.

Expenditure is first regarded as spending on the first set of goods and services – the output of the production sector. Expenditure on GDP is identical with GDP as output as a matter of double-entry book-keeping. It is got from total domestic expenditure in two steps. The first step is to add exports of goods and services from the domestic economy to give an aggregate with the label of *total final expenditure*. Since both total domestic expenditure and exports have import contents – and since all imports appear in one or the other – all that is needed at the second step is to deduct total imports of goods and services to get expenditure on GDP:

> Total final expenditure = total domestic
>   expenditure *plus* exports of goods
>   and services   (E)
> Expenditure on GDP = total final expenditure
>   *less* imports of goods and services

The concept of total final expenditure is a very wide one. It is the sum of all consumer goods and services purchased by nationals, of all exports bought by foreigners at whatever stage of production they had reached on export, and of all purchases of fixed capital goods for installation in the domestic economy, together with increases in stocks (regarded as purchased by the stockholders). It is to be contrasted with *intermediate expenditure* as the sum of spending on intermediate goods and services. These are goods and services which are both bought and resold (in the same or changed form) within the domestic economy in the year in question.

Expenditure on GDP is identically equal to GDP as output. Hence the difference between GDP and total domestic expenditure is by (E) the excess of exports over imports of goods and services. The difference is positive or negative according to whether exports are greater or less than imports. When exports exceed imports, GDP is larger than total domestic expenditure. This case is the one assumed in Fig. 2.3 in drawing the line in the third column above that drawn across the first two columns. It can equally well happen that exports are less than imports; the line in the third column is then to be drawn below that across the other two.

GDP is converted to GNP in (C) above by the addition of net property income from abroad. A similar addition to (E) gives:

Expenditure on GNP = total domestic expenditure
　　plus exports of goods and services
　　less imports of goods and services　　　　　　　　　(F)
　　plus net property income from abroad

This aggregate of expenditures is by definition identical with GNP as it appears as sums of outputs and of incomes at the foot of the first two columns of Fig. 2.3.

The official national accounts make much use of expenditure as the sum of what is spent on the goods and services which make up output. The alternative concept is still of considerable if subsidiary interest: purchases by nationals out of income, including imports but excluding exports. It is used in the national accounts, notably for expenditure out of total personal income (2.4 below) as well as out of gross national income as considered here.

Gross national expenditure is the sum of the great variety of purchases made by UK nationals out of gross national income: all purchases, including imports, by nationals as consumers and their gross expenditure on investment in capital assets of all kinds, both at home and abroad. A further item needs to be added to make the total identical with gross national income: net transfers to abroad. As with all such aggregates, transfers are excluded from gross national income. Those between nationals also cancel out in aggregate expenditure; a gift, for example, simply transfers purchases from one person to another within the total. This is not the case when the transfers are to or from foreigners. Transfers made by nationals to foreigners are partly offset against transfers received from abroad but leaving a balance – net transfers to abroad – to be met out of income.

The last column of Fig. 2.3 is completed by building up total domestic expenditure into gross national expenditure. Total domestic expenditure includes consumers' expenditure and domestic investment by nationals; hence expenditure by nationals on investment abroad, as well as net transfers to abroad, need to be added. On the other hand, total domestic expenditure includes domestic investment by foreigners and this must be deducted. Hence two net additions have to be made; one is net transfers to abroad and the other is investment abroad by UK nationals net of investment in the UK by foreigners. Net investment abroad has to be given the wide interpretation it gets in the UK balance of payments: the acquisition of overseas assets of all kinds of UK nationals net of corresponding assets acquired by foreigners in the UK. Assets cover the whole range from such physical items as mines and property overseas to holdings of foreign currencies in overseas banks or in exchange reserves. Hence:

> Gross national expenditure = total domestic
> expenditure *plus* net transfers to   (G)
> abroad *plus* net investment abroad

It is as well to check that gross national expenditure, as a total composed of purchases by nationals and given by (G), is identical with expenditure on GNP given by (F) and hence with GNP as output. This confirms the identities in the last row of Fig. 2.3. The check picks up the current account balance as struck in the UK balance of payments and interpreted as net investment abroad (5.6 below):

> Net investment abroad = export of goods and
> services *less* imports of goods and
> services *plus* net property income   (H)
> from abroad *less* net transfers to
> abroad

The substitution of (H) into (G) gives (F) and the check is accomplished.

A word of warning: the qualification 'net' is used in the national accounts in two rather different senses. They are both well established; they must be accepted and lived with. One use is very specific: it distinguishes between a gross aggregate such as GDP before depreciation and the corresponding net aggregate NDP after depreciation. Other uses are more general and serve simply to show that two related figures have been subtracted one from the other. So net may be used in an accounting context to indicate an excess of credits over debits: net interest, for example, is the difference between interest receipts and payments. The examples met above relate to international transactions: net property income from abroad, net transfers to abroad, net investment abroad. Another instance is the term 'net product' some-times used for value added. This term is avoided in Figs 2.2 and 2.3 because of the awkward result: gross domestic product equals the sum of net products. The 'gross' here refers to one concept and the 'net' to another. A final example: net indirect taxes is a term often employed (2.3 below) for the excess of taxes on expenditure over subsidies.

Relevant references to *Sources and Methods* are: the concept of the production boundary, pp. 44–5; the definition of UK residents, pp. 436–8; property income and transfers from and to abroad, pp. 445–8; net investment abroad, pp. 448–9.

2.3 Treatment of Government

The three boxes of Fig. 2.2 and the three columns of Fig. 2.3 assume no government, an assumption now to be dropped. Public corporations (nationalised industries) present no problem in this context. They fall within their appropriate industries in the output box and contribute income both from employment and as trading profits or surpluses to the income box. In the third box, consumers' expenditure includes pur-chases from the public corporations and gross domestic investment includes their capital formation. The same is true of the trading departments (e.g. council housing) of central and local government.

The problems arise in arranging the national accounts to handle the non-trading activities of government. They are of two kinds, those relating to government as a service 'industry' and those created by the existence of taxes and subsidies.

The list of domestic industries in the output box needs to be extended by the insertion of non-trading government among the service industries and by the specification of the appropriate value added. Government services comprise public administration, defence, public health and education; these may be lumped together into a single industry or split into several such industries. The services are provided to the community, usually without charge, and it is neither practicable nor desirable to value them in the same way as the services of cinemas, solicitors or hairdressers. Instead the assumption is made that the value of the service equals the total outgoings of non-trading government on labour, services and materials. On subtraction of inputs, the value added is the sum of all wages and salaries paid to civil servants, including members of HM Forces and employees of local authorities, in non-trading government. There is one adjustment: the addition of imputed charges for depreciation of non-trading property owned and occupied by government (2.9 below). These are also the entries for non-trading government in the income box.

The contribution of non-trading government to total domestic expenditure is two-fold. Part of gross domestic investment is made by government in building and equipping schools, hospitals and other non-trading property. Part of consumption expenditure by nationals is their purchases of the community services supplied by government as valued, on the assumption made above, by the outgoings of non-trading government. The latter are classified as *government final consumption* and total domestic expenditure shows them separately:

> Total domestic expenditure = consumers'
> expenditure *plus* government final
> consumption *plus* gross domestic
> investment   (A)

The last item consists of all capital formation, both fixed and as increases in stocks, in the private and in the public sector.

A different set of problems arises from the effect of taxes and subsidies on prices. There are two types of valuation used in the national accounts. Valuation *at factor cost* is directly applied to domestic product as output and income; it is out of values added that the factors are remunerated. Valuation *at market prices* – at the prices actually paid by purchasers – is the way in which total domestic expenditure and exports, and their sum as total final expenditure, are directly expressed.

The difference between the two valuations arises because of the ancient practice whereby governments levy taxes on expenditure and of the more modern habit of paying subsidies to reduce prices. Taxes on expenditure are commonly called indirect taxes and subsidies are regarded as negative indirect taxes. For any item or group of items, the excess of valuation at market prices over that at factor cost is:

> Net indirect taxes = taxes on expenditure *less* subsidies

Most indirect taxes are levied by the central government and they range from VAT and car tax to various excise duties, but some, notably rates, are paid to local authorities. Subsidies are paid to farmers, transport operators and others, and in respect of housing activities by local government.

So the components and totals of gross domestic product are valued primarily at factor cost. But they can be written at market prices by simply adding the relevant figure of net indirect taxes. Similarly, total domestic and final expenditures, and their components, are usually obtained at market prices; the values can then be reduced to factor cost by deduction of the appropriate net indirect taxes.

It is convenient to have the aggregates of the national accounts both at factor cost and at market prices. Factor cost valuations are especially relevant to any consideration of the distribution of resources; values at market prices are to be used in assessing economic welfare. For an economist's discussion, see appendix note F in J. R. Hicks, *The Social Framework*, 4th edn (Oxford: OUP, 1971).

In a detailed specification of values at factor cost and at market prices, it is important to be clear on the treatment of net indirect taxes on items entering into external trade. Total final expenditure is an aggregate of wide scope which is commonly obtained at market prices and then reduced to factor cost by the deduction of a comprehension figure for net indirect taxes. Start with (A) for total domestic expenditure, taken at market prices, and add exports of goods and services, also at market prices. These are the values of exports shown, inclusive of indirect taxes net of subsidies, in the current account of the balance of payments (5.2 and 5.3 below). They are free on board (fob) valuations of goods, as in the published data on merchandise trade, together with services valued at the time of transaction. All the components of total domestic expenditure and of exports include indirect taxes and subsidies and between them they account for all net indirect taxes. Hence:

Total final expenditure at market prices = total
    domestic expenditure *plus* exports of
    goods and services, both at market
    prices   (B)
Total final expenditure at factor cost = total
    final expenditure at market prices
    less net indirect taxes*

* In total including indirect taxes (net of subsidies) on imports.

On the other hand, the reduction of a component of total final expenditure to factor cost requires the subtraction of only that part of the total of net indirect taxes relevant to the component. For example, total domestic expenditure at factor cost is arrived at by deducting all indirect taxes (net of subsidies) except those levied on exports of goods and services.

All the components of total final expenditure have import contents and between them they add to total imports of goods and services. A part of the total of net indirect taxes, and indeed a substantial part, consists of those levied on imports, a fact indicated by the footnote to (B). GDP as output and income is got from total final expenditure by the deduction of imports of goods and services, on formula (E) of 2.2 above. The basic valuation of GDP is at factor cost and it can be raised to market prices by adding net indirect taxes. The question arises: should the net indirect taxes here include or exclude those on imports?

The convenient choice, to make life easier in handling the national accounts, is to include the total of all indirect taxes in GDP at market prices. The switch from market prices to factor cost, by subtraction of all net indirect taxes, would then be the same for GDP as for total final expenditure in (B).

This is the choice made in the official national accounts of the UK. It follows that, when imports are deducted from total final expenditure to get GDP (both at market prices), net indirect taxes must be left in: i.e. not deducted with imports. Imports of goods and services need to be valued before indirect taxes and subsidies, exactly as they appear in the current account of the balance of payments: free on board (fob) for goods and transaction values for services. This is very convenient; both exports and imports are valued as in the UK balance of payments and come straight from this source of data.

The derivation of GDP on the choice made is:

GDP at market prices* = total final expenditure
    less imports of goods and services
GDP at factor cost = GDP at market prices *less*
    net indirect taxes*
(C)

* Including indirect taxes (net of subsidies) on imports.

Here imports are valued as in the balance of payments before indirect taxes and subsidies. These net indirect taxes fall as indicated in the footnote.

If the alternative choice were made, then the imports subtracted in the first equation of (C) would be inclusive of net indirect taxes levied on them. GDP at market prices would be smaller by the amount of net indirect taxes on imports. The deduction in the second equation of (C) would be of net indirect taxes, not in total, but excluding those on imports, so giving (as it must) the same figure for GDP valued at factor cost. This may be more logical but it makes for awkward handling and it is not adopted in the official national accounts.

2.4 Main Aggregates to be Estimated

Before proceeding to consider statistical estimation in practice we can recapitulate briefly. At the national level in Fig. 2.3 the gross totals of output, income and expenditure are identical by definition and expenditure is viewed in two ways:

Gross national output ≡ gross national income ≡
    expenditure on gross national output ≡   (A)
    gross national expenditure

The valuations in (A) may be all at factor cost; or, with the addition of the total indirect taxes (net of subsidies) to each, they may be at market prices. The first three of (A) are the three aspects of a single concept: the totality of goods and services produced by UK nationals. In 2.2, they are given the single and convenient label: GNP for *gross national product*. The last of (A) is different and relates to the totality of goods and services purchased (rather than produced) by UK nationals out of gross national income. By formula (G) of 2.2, it is the sum of domestic purchases (total domestic expenditure) and of net investment abroad and net transfers to abroad. It is usually valued at market prices and it can be stored away for later use (9.4 below).

At the domestic level the line drawn across the first two columns of Fig. 2.3 indicates the identity by definition of the gross totals of output and income. These totals are also identical, by definition, with aggregate expenditure on gross output. So:

Gross domestic output ≡ gross domestic income
    ≡ expenditure on gross domestic output   (B)

These are three versions of a single concept given the label GDP for *gross domestic product*. They can be at factor cost or, by the addition of the total of net indirect taxes, at market prices.

Hence, by (B), there are three identical measures of GDP in total at factor cost. The addition of net property income from abroad converts them into three identical measures of GNP in total at factor cost, the first three entries in (A). Since property income to and from abroad attracts no indirect taxes or subsidies, the valuation at factor cost, equally of GDP and GNP, is raised to market prices by the addition of a single figure: the total of indirect taxes net of subsidies. All measures of GDP relate to the totality of goods and services produced in the domestic economy and all measures of GNP to the goods and services produced by nationals. The position is summarised in Fig. 2.4.

The basic aggregate in the national accounts is *GDP at factor cost*. Once this is estimated, three other gross aggregates follow, as shown in Fig. 2.4. There are then four corresponding net aggregates obtained after allowance for depreciation, i.e. by deduction of an estimate for capital consumption. The national accounts assume, at least as a matter

	Domestic	National
At factor cost	GDP at factor cost $= X$	GNP at factor cost $= X + x$
At market prices	GDP at market prices $= X + y$	GNP at market prices $= X + x + y$

x = Net property income from abroad
y = Net indirect taxes

Fɪɢ. 2.4 Four gross product aggregates

of convenience, that property income to and from abroad is always given after depreciation. It follows that the same figure of capital consumption is used for all aggregates. In practice, the only net aggregate commonly derived is:

NNP at factor cost = GNP at factor cost *less* capital consumption.

This is the economists' concept of *net national income*, the income flow to UK nationals after provision for maintaining capital intact. The nature of the required estimate of capital consumption, in total and by main industrial groups, is described in *Sources and Methods*, pp. 16–17 and 383–7.

When GDP is viewed as income, as in Fig. 2.2 and 2.3, the contributions of companies, public corporations and trading enterprises of government are rent and gross profits or surpluses. Dividends and interest paid out make no appearances as such; they are regarded as transfers to stockholders. There is an alternative approach making use of the concept of income received, an approach which is especially relevant when the national accounts are developed into sector accounts.

The economy is divided into four main *sectors*: personal, corporate, government and overseas. Each sector is taken as grouping together those entities, e.g. persons or companies, with a specific economic activity. Then, for each sector, three *accounts* are drawn up in the kind of way followed by accountants in business: operating or trading; income/expenditure or appropriation; capital or saving/investment. Some of the sector accounts are considered later (see 4.1 below) and a fuller description is in *Sources and Methods*, pp. 19–28. A more elaborate system is developed by G. Stuvel, *Systems of Social Accounts* (Oxford: OUP, 1965).

The personal sector comprises all persons, whether in households or not, together with unincorporated private enterprises and non-profitmaking bodies, as a convenient convention in the national accounts. In the main sector account (4.2 below) personal income is set off against expenditure. The income side of this account comprises all incomes actually received and the total is given the label *total personal income*. Apart from some minor modifications, made later, the definition is:

Total personal income = income from employment
and self-employment *plus* rent,
dividends and net interest received   (C)
plus current grants received

The current grants are mainly from government: a great range of benefits under national insurance and such items as family allowances, rent rebates and grants to universities. Current donations from outside the personal sector to non-profitmaking bodies should also be covered and in practice current transfers from companies to charities are included as far as identifiable in Inland Revenue data.

Total personal income is obtained gross and at factor cost so that (e.g.) self-employment income is before depreciation. It is at the national level, including property income received by the personal sector from abroad but not property income paid abroad. Its nearest correspondent among product aggregates is GNP at factor cost, from which it differs in two respects: it excludes some income attributable to UK nationals (e.g. undistributed profits of companies) while it includes transfers (current grants and national debt interest) omitted from GNP. The adjustment from one to the other comprises both additions and subtractions; in practice total personal income is lower than GNP at factor cost in most years but it can be greater (e.g. around 1975).

As they have developed over the years, the national accounts of the UK and of many other developed countries have increasingly concentrated on the build up of GDP at factor cost. Once this is done the switch to other gross aggregates is easily made (Fig. 2.4). The *Blue Book* continues to carry the title *national income and expenditure*, exactly as used in the original White Paper, Cmd 6261 of 1941. This suggests an analysis of expenditure on purchases out of income, something which is indeed in the national accounts, notably Table 1.3 of the *Blue Book* on personal income and expenditure. What is certainly true, however, is that the leading Tables 1.1 and 1.2 of the *Blue Book* and much of the supporting detail relate to income from and expenditure on GDP at factor cost.

2.5 Three Measures of GDP at Factor Cost

The implication of identities (B) of 2.4 above is that one and the same total of GDP at factor cost can be reached by three routes. The routes differ in the components added together to give the total.

The *output measure* is the sum of values added in the various industries, including government services, into which the domestic economy is divided, all at factor cost and before depreciation. For the industries of the census of production, values added (net outputs) are as thrown up in the census, adjusted to ensure that all inputs of services are deducted, subject only to a reservation on the treatment of financial services (2.7 below). Similar values added are estimated for other industries.

The *income measure* is got by the addition of all factor incomes generated in the domestic economy whether they go to nationals or to foreigners. The incomes are partly from employment, self-employment and rents and partly from gross trading profits of companies and gross trading surpluses in the public sector. Rent is estimated and shown separately as a matter of convenience (2.9 below).

The *expenditure measure* is the total of all expenditures on GDP as output at factor cost, reached at the end of a long chain of valuations at market prices, reduced to factor cost in a final adjustment. The main part of the exercise is the build up of total domestic expenditure as the sum of all current expenditure by consumers and government and of all gross investment expenditure in the domestic economy. The adjustments to expenditure on GDP at factor cost are those of formulae (B) and (C) of 2.3 above. They use exports of goods and services including net indirect taxes and imports of goods and services excluding net indirect taxes, exactly as provided in the UK balance of payments. As explained in 2.3 above, this method implies that the final reduction to factor cost is by subtraction of the total of all net indirect taxes.

The double-entry book-keeping which lies behind these computations ensures that the three measures are of one and the same concept, GDP at factor cost. As a matter of statistical practice the three totals can turn out to be different – but only because of the well-known fact that statistical estimates contain errors, duplications and omissions of one kind or another.

In UK practice there are two, not three, basically independent estimates of GDP at factor cost. One is from the side of income and the other from expenditures. An estimate from the output side is made, but it is simply a rearrangement of the income estimate by means of a cross-classification of the data by industry and type of income, as shown in Table 3.1 of the *Blue Book*. This makes use of the fact that the value added in an industry is the sum of factor incomes generated in the industry.

Hence UK estimates produce two totals of GDP at factor cost, one from income/output data and one from the expenditure side. They are different from each other and from the 'correct' figure because of statistical errors. Some assessment of the errors involved is given in the section on reliability in *Sources and Methods* pp. 39–42.

Two questions arise. Both estimates are subject to error: can an estimate be arrived at for the error in each? The answer is: no. Since this doesn't work, can the relative errors be assessed so that one total can be taken as nearer to the 'correct' figure than the other? The answer is again: no. A compromise is needed; that adopted is described on p. 108 of the 1979 *Blue Book*:

Two estimates of the gross domestic product are built up from largely independent data on income and final expenditure. The *residual error* – the difference between the two independent estimates – is presented as though it were an item (positive or negative) of income. This is purely for convenience of presentation and does not imply that the estimates of expenditure are necessarily superior in accuracy to the estimates of income.

The expenditure estimate is left alone and the other shown with a residual error:

Expenditure estimate of GDP = income/output estimate of GDP
    + residual error

If the double-entry book-keeping technique could be carried through completely – quite impossible in practice – it would still not remove the statistical errors of estimate. It would simply ensure that the same errors, which could be large, appear in the two totals; the totals would agree and the residual error would be nil. The common total would still not be the 'correct' figure. Equally a small residual error does not necessarily imply that the totals are near to the 'correct' figure.

The residual error may be positive or negative. It was negative in the UK estimates for 1969 and 1970. Subsequently and more usually it has been positive; the expenditure estimate is commonly the greater of the two.

2.6 Components of GDP at Factor Cost

The estimates of GDP achieve total aggregates at the peak of a massive structure built up brick by brick from almost countless detail. In a genuine sense it is the components, and the vast detail each comprises, which matter.

On the income/output side, the land, labour and capital of the economists still provide the framework (2.1 above). Income from land and buildings is shown separately in the national accounts as rent; the sources of data are different from those of other incomes and there is the problem of owner-occupancy (2.9 below). Incomes from labour, and from the provision of capital and enterprise, are shown in summary tables in the two clear-cut categories of employment income and gross trading profits or surpluses, together with a mixed category of self-employment income. There are several sources of data, e.g. accounts of public corporations and government trading enterprises. The largest single source is the Inland Revenue and their tax assessments on companies and on individual taxpayers. This source needs to be supplemented by other data, e.g. those obtained from companies by the Business Statistics Office (BSO) and on earnings by the Department of Employment.

The use of Inland Revenue data as a main source has one consequence: additions need to be made both for earnings below tax limits and for the understatement of income in tax returns. There is some understatement of income in PAYE records, e.g. for domestic servants, and in tax returns by companies on profits; appropriate additions are made to allow for the shortfall. The main understatement arises, however, in returns of self-employment income and this is where the major adjustments occur. The extent of economic activity avoiding tax, sometimes called the 'black economy', may be reflected in the size of the residual error (excess of expenditure estimate over income estimate). This became large in the 1970s.

On the expenditure side, there are statistical difficulties in the specialised area of exports and imports in the balance of payments (5.2 and 5.3 below). More formidable problems arise in the estimation of total domestic expenditure at market prices. Consumers' expenditure is the major component both in size and in the vast variety of detail. The sources of data are diverse: National Food Surveys, Family Expenditure Surveys, statistics of retail sales, the returns of Customs and Excise, and many others. There are so many, indeed, that there are major risks of overlap and of omission; much statistical effort is devoted to insuring against these risks. Government final consumption is easier: the sources are government accounts, rearranged extensively to be consistent with national income concepts. Finally, capital formation in fixed assets and in stocks is derived largely from BSO and from government accounts. Returns made to BSO are geared to company accounts used in tax assessments so that consistency is maintained in principle (e.g.) with profits on the income side.

A detailed account of the estimates occupies much of the space in *Sources and Methods*, following a summary on pp. 32–42.

The main components of each measure of GDP at factor cost are set out in the three boxes of Fig. 2.5, a developed form of Fig. 2.2, with illustrative figures for 1978 from the 1979 *Blue Book*. It can be seen that there are two different totals, one from the income/output side and one from expenditures; they are squared off by putting the residual error on the income/output side.

We can conclude with a brief recapitulation and amplification of the components of GDP at factor cost shown in Fig. 2.5. The *income box*

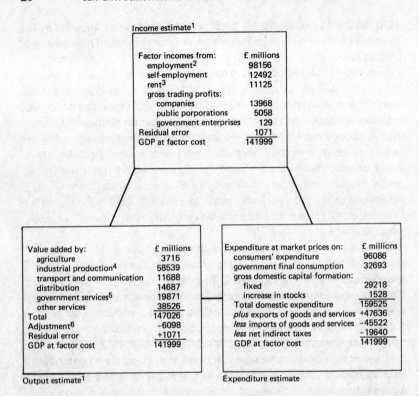

Income estimate[1]

Factor incomes from:	£ millions
employment[2]	98156
self-employment	12492
rent[3]	11125
gross trading profits:	
companies	13968
public porporations	5058
government enterprises	129
Residual error	1071
GDP at factor cost	141999

Value added by:	£ millions
agriculture	3715
industrial production[4]	58539
transport and communication	11688
distribution	14687
government services[5]	19871
other services	38526
Total	147026
Adjustment[6]	−6098
Residual error	+1071
GDP at factor cost	141999

Output estimate[1]

Expenditure at market prices on:	£ millions
consumers' expenditure	96086
government final consumption	32693
gross domestic capital formation:	
fixed	29218
increase in stocks	1528
Total domestic expenditure	159525
plus exports of goods and services	+47636
less imports of goods and services	−45522
less net indirect taxes	−19640
GDP at factor cost	141999

Expenditure estimate

[1] After provision for stock appreciation (2.8).
[2] Including employers' contributions to national insurance etc. (2.7).
[3] Including imputed rents and charges (2.9).
[4] Mining, manufacturing, construction, gas, electricity and water.
[5] Public administration, defence, public health and education.
[6] For financial services (2.7).

FIG. 2.5 GDP at factor cost 1978

starts with what is by far the largest component: employment income in the form of wages, salaries and pay of HM Forces. This is the sum of all payments to employees, with certain additions for income in kind and for national insurance and pension schemes (2.7 below). A separate figure can be got for HM Forces pay but it is no longer practicable to distinguish wages from salaries. Next, the mixed category of self-employment income is the sum of the incomes of three rather different groups:

Farmers: all commercial holdings including agricultural companies. Professional workers, alone or in partnership, excluding employees. Other sole traders, alone or in partnership, excluding employees: e.g. shop-keepers, salesmen on commission.

After showing rent separately the box ends with gross trading profits or surpluses in three types of enterprise. Companies include financial institutions, so that such unincorporated bodies as building societies come here (and not in the personal sector). Public corporations are a group which varies over time. A few changes are out to the private sector, e.g. the Atomic Energy Authority (1971). Many more are in from the government or private sector, e.g. the Post Office (1961) and British Aerospace (1977). Others are newly created by legislation, e.g. the British National Oil Corporation (1976). Government trading enterprises are mainly run by local authorities, e.g. transport, council housing. The Forestry Commission is one of the few left in central government.

The *output box* is relatively simple: a rearrangement of incomes to give values added in an appropriately specified list of industries.

The *expenditure box* shows total domestic expenditure split between current expenditures, by consumers and by government, and gross domestic investment, whether in such fixed assets as plant, equipment and vehicles or as increases in stocks and work in progress. The line drawn between current goods and services and those which are additions to wealth is somewhat arbitrary; consumer durables shade off into capital goods. The conventional line is drawn so that capital goods include dwellings and all non-trading property such as schools and hospitals as well as the vast range of trading plant and equipment. Hence consumers' expenditure covers rents of dwellings and purchases of all consumer durables except new housing. It also includes rentals paid to the service trades of car hire and TV and radio renting. The purchase of the cars, TV and radio sets by the rental firms is part of capital formation.

The box for expenditure also specifies the three adjustments to convert total domestic expenditure into GDP at factor cost. There are two intermediate stops in the conversion process: total final expenditure and GDP at market prices. It is important to remember not only how the conversion proceeds on the formulae (B) and (C) of 2.3 above, but also precisely what is in the totals at the different stages. Fig. 2.6 is designed to serve as an aid to memory.

Aggregate	Expenditure on			
	Domestic output Home sales	Exports	Imports	Net indirect taxes
Total domestic expenditure at market prices	√	—	*√	*√
Total final expenditure at market prices	√	√	√	√
GDP at market prices	√	√	—	√
GDP at factor cost	√	√	—	—

* Excluding import content of exports and net indirect taxes levied on exports

Fig. 2.6 Content of expenditure aggregates

2.7 Complications and Conventions

The concept of UK national income is: the sum of *money* incomes received by UK nationals from *current* economic activity. From the two words in italics it follows that, strictly, all non-money incomes and all transfers are excluded. The question is: how strictly?

There is no difficulty about the omission of *transfers* from income/output aggregates. They represent the passing of money which is not in response to current economic activity. They may redistribute the national income but do not add to the total. One example, transfers to and from abroad, has already been noted (2.2 above). Other examples are: gifts and legacies; unemployment and sickness benefits; rent rebates and supplementary benefits; grants to universities and students; current grants from companies to charities.

The treatment of *interest on loans* raises some problems. One item is regarded in the national accounts as a transfer: national debt interest. The national debt has been built up from past government activity, mainly in fighting wars, and it has nothing to do with current economic matters. Otherwise interest is best viewed not so much as a transfer, but as the return derived from the provision of financial services (e.g.) by banks to business. Payments and receipts then cancel out in the sum of values added by industry as for all intermediate goods and services.

It is easy to agree that *pensions* of all kinds are excluded as arising from past rather than current activity. It follows that the national income must include all contributions to the national insurance funds from which state pensions, and other benefits, are paid. Employee contributions are in wages and salaries; employers' contributions are not and need to be added. The same holds for current contributions to superannuation and pension schemes. When the schemes are not funded, current pensions are taken as contributions.

The funds of *life assurance and superannuation schemes* are considered in the national accounts as the collective property of the policy-holders and of the members of the schemes. The accounts of the personal sector need to be adjusted appropriately. The income of the schemes (apart from premiums) is included in the entry in personal income for rent, dividends and net interest. Consumers' expenditure includes an item for the administrative costs of the schemes. These are payments by consumers for a specific service, that of the provision of life cover. See *Sources and Methods*, pp. 100, 101 and 181.

The transactions involved in *secondhand dealing* contain two elements. In the buying and selling of (e.g.) a used car, one element is the price fixed for the car and the other is the profit of the dealer. The second is part of the national income, a payment for a service. The first is not related to current activity; it is a transfer from buyer to seller. As with all transfers, it adds nothing to national income though it may affect the calculation of components. If the buyer and seller are private persons, then the deal cancels out in consumers' expenditure in the expenditure estimate of GDP. If the car is sold by a business user to an individual, then a positive entry in consumers' expenditure is matched by an equal but negative entry in capital formation.

The exclusion of *non-money incomes*, if carried through strictly, would raise serious problems of comparability of national income over time or between countries and regions. The services of housewives and the do-it-yourself work by householders are among the non-money items excluded. This has become accepted practice though it implies that national income falls if a man marries his housekeeper or paints his house himself instead of calling in the local builder.

The point at which such exclusions become unacceptable is soon reached. Some incomes usually paid in money may be arranged on a non-cash basis. Examples of these *incomes in kind* are: board and lodging of domestic servants, miners' concessionary coal, own produce consumed by farmers, a bank manager's rent-free flat. The housing market provides an even more important case where some services are paid for in cash and similar ones involve no money passing. Many dwellings are rented and the income of the owners, after repairs and maintenance, is shown under 'rent' in national income. Other properties are owner-occupied and housing services are supplied by the owner to himself as occupier, but without charge.

If such non-money items were excluded, national income would fall as it becomes economically or socially desirable – or just fashionable – to take income in kind or to buy one's own house, with no real change in services rendered. In the interests of comparability, therefore, incomes in kind are given *imputed values* in money, on the basis of a comparison with similar incomes in cash, and added to national income. In particular, imputed rents are estimated for owner-occupied dwellings. The situation, both for dwellings and for other forms of property which are owner-occupied, is examined in 2.9 below.

Imputation, in effect, involves the creation of a piece of double-entry book-keeping. On the income side, the imputed value of miners' coal is added to employment income and imputed rent for owner-occupied dwellings to rent income. On the output side, the items are cross-classified to the relevant industry, here coalmining and an industry given the label 'ownership of dwellings'. The other entry in the invented piece of book-keeping is on the expenditure side. In the two examples, the entries are in consumers' expenditure, under fuel for miners' coal and housing for the imputed rent. The miner is regarded, in this book-keeping exercise, as buying coal from himself; the owner-occupier is viewed as paying rent as occupier to himself as owner. Consumers' expenditure also includes a residual category for 'income in kind not included elsewhere' to sweep in cases when no specific allocation can be made. An example is food and clothing supplied to the armed forces, in income under employment income and in the residual category on the expenditure side.

A description of the coverage of *employment income* must, therefore, include references to income in kind and to national insurance and pension schemes. Suitably abbreviated, the definition of the *Blue Book* is: wages and salaries, before deduction of income tax or insurance contributions, *plus* income in kind *less* expenses of employment; pay in cash and kind of HM Forces; employers' contributions to the national insurance scheme and to superannuation and other pension funds.

There is a matter arising out of what has been said above about interest on loans; it requires a conventional *adjustment for financial services*. The main income of (e.g.) a bank is obtained by charging more for loans than it pays to depositors. Net interest receipts are included in the value added by the banking and finance industry, as the return on financial services rendered to other industries. These services are intermediate, not final. Hence the values added by industries using the services should be obtained after deduction of the net interest payments. This is not yet possible with available data. A compromise is adopted:

net interest payments are left in the value added by the industry of banking and finance but not deducted from other values added. The resulting duplication in the sum of values added is corrected by an adjustment for financial services separately at the end, as at the bottom of the output box of Fig. 2.5.

2.8 Stock Appreciation

Investment in the form of increases in stocks and work in progress is included in the expenditure estimate of GDP. To relate properly to current economic activity, this must be the *physical* increase in stocks and work in progress valued at current market prices during the year. Call it for short:

Value of physical increase in stocks   (A)

where 'stocks' are taken always to include work in progress. The valuation should strictly be at prices ruling during the year as stocks change; but it can be taken, as an approximation, at the average price of the year for each commodity stocked.

The income and output measures of GDP include gross trading profits calculated on standard accounting methods as accepted by the Inland Revenue for tax purposes. Profits come from the part of value added by enterprises not paid out (e.g. as wages and salaries) to factors of production. In its turn, value added is got by taking sales and closing book values of stocks and by subtracting purchases and opening stocks. The contribution of increases in stocks to gross trading profits, and hence to GDP as income and output, is the excess of closing over opening *book values*. Call it for short

Increase in book value of stocks   (B)

Here, as in (A), stocks include work in progress.

(A) is incorporated in the expenditure measure, (B) in the income and output measure of GDP. The first is correct; the second is inconsistent and needs to be put right. The adjustment to the income and output measures is: first deduct (B) as incorrectly included and then add the correct (A). The net deduction is (B)–(A), given the label *stock appreciation*. It represents that part of the increase in book values of stocks which arises from price movements rather than from physical changes in stocks held. It is positive when prices are generally rising, the case usually found in practice. It is possible, however, for prices generally to fall and hence to make stock appreciation negative.

At times of inflation, when prices rise rapidly, stock appreciation is positive and large, and may well convert a negative (A) into a positive (B):

$$(B) = (A) \ plus \ \text{stock appreciation}$$

It is quite possible for a situation of declining stocks to be disguised by increasing book values created by inflation.

Estimates of stock appreciation in the national accounts are necessarily approximate. This is partly because the variety of materials and products held in stock, and of work in progress, make it necessary to work with values deflated for price movements rather than with physical changes. But it is mainly because of the great mixture of different methods used by accountants in arriving at book values of stocks held by enterprises, a mixture of actual costs and of standard or realisable values. For an account of the concepts, problems and methods of estimation of stock appreciation, see *Sources and Methods*, pp. 16–18, 391–3 and 401–5.

The estimates are obtained in total, for main industrial groups and for trading profits and self-employment income separately. The adjustment of GDP as income or output for stock appreciation can be done *either* by subtracting total stock appreciation from the unadjusted estimate of GDP *or* by separate deduction of stock appreciation from each of the main components of GDP. The first is done in some *Blue Book* tabulations, as illustrated in 3.4 below. The second is used in the income and output boxes of Fig. 2.5.

2.9 Treatment of Rent

The ownership of land and buildings, if they are rented, gives rise to an income which, after maintenance costs, appears under 'rent' in the income box of Fig. 2.5. There are problems when the property is owner-occupied and they need to be explored.

The treatment of owner-occupied *trading property* (except farms) is a matter for the operating account of the enterprise. In the estimation of gross trading profits for national income, it does not matter whether a rent is imputed or not, for it would appear equally on the two sides of the account (as an income and an expenditure) and cancel out. Hence no imputation of rent is needed.

For *dwellings and farms* which are owner-occupied, as for those provided rent-free as an income in kind, imputed rents are estimated on the basis of similar rented property. Imputed and actual rents alike appear under 'rent' in the income box of Fig. 2.5.

There remains other owner-occupied *non-trading property*, a large group of properties such as schools, hospitals, town halls, university buildings and properties of charities. These used to be treated like dwellings and imputed rents estimated. Present practice is to ignore the rent income which might be thought to arise from the ownership of such properties – not a very meaningful concept. Instead an imputed charge for capital consumption is estimated and added to an income measure of GDP. Otherwise too much would be removed when a single figure for total capital consumption – all that can be got – is deducted to give the net aggregate. Such charges are entered as 'imputed charge for consumption of non-trading capital', an additional item in the income box of Fig. 2.5.

Rent incomes need to be allocated to the appropriate industries in the output box of Fig. 2.5. These are agriculture for actual or imputed farm rents, ownership of dwelling for actual or imputed rents of dwellings, real estate for other rented property, government or other services for imputed charges for owner-occupied non-trading property.

On the double-entry book-keeping system, there are rent expenditures to be slotted in. The services of trading properties (including farms) are intermediate, not final commodities. Their rents do not appear in the expenditure box of Fig. 2.5; they simply disappear in operating accounts. What does get in the box is all rents on rented dwellings and non-trading properties, all imputed rents of owner-occupied dwellings and all imputed charges for owner-occupied non-trading properties. They are included either under housing in consumers' expenditure or (for government non-trading property) under government final consumption.

3 Main Aggregates: Tabulations

3.1 Introduction

The tabulation of this chapter are designed to show the way in which GDP at factor cost, or one of its variants, is built up from its main components on the output, income and expenditure sides. They are based on what has been said in 2.5 and 2.6 and on the boxes of Figure 2.5 above. Annual data for 1975 and 1978 from the 1979 *Blue Book* are used for illustration; the 1975 figures are firm, and those for 1978 provisional. The tabulations come from some of the summary tables of the *Blue Book*, mainly from Table 1.1 for the expenditure components, Table 1.2 for incomes and Table 1.10 for estimates of output by industry.

The years 1975–8 are a period both of considerable inflation and of recovery from depression. In order to quantify changes over the period, some of the tabulations show appropriate percentages. One type of percentage is simple: a total or component in 1978 expressed as a percentage of the corresponding figure in 1975. This suffers from the fact that, being based on current prices, the percentages reflect the combined result of a recovery in real terms and of inflationary price movements. The way to separate these two factors appears later (Chapters 6–9); meanwhile it is of interest to compare, one with another, the percentage increases shown by various components. A second type of percentage has some advantages in this respect: the percentage distribution of a total over its components in 1978 as compared with 1975. To the extent that inflation affects components in much the same way, the changing percentage distribution tends to show up real movements.

As has already been said, similar but less extensive data are published quarterly in the articles which appear in *Economic Trends* in January, April, July and October each year. Tables 1 and 2 of these articles give GDP quarterly from the expenditure and income sides but not in terms of output by industry. In the handling of quarterly as opposed to yearly figures there is the problem of allowing for seasonal variation.

Components of GDP are commonly influenced by seasonal factors ranging from the weather to the incidence of holidays. Published series overcome the difficulty by giving quarterly figures both in the original form and seasonally adjusted. Well-known statistical techniques, usually the X-11 variant of the Shiskin method developed in the United States, are used to make the seasonal adjustments.

3.2 Four Gross Product Aggregates

Figure 2.4 above relates the basic aggregate of GDP at factor cost to the three variants obtained by switching from the domestic to the national level and by raising factor cost to market prices. Table 3.1 sets out the four aggregates in 1975 and in 1978, the adjustments being as shown in Table 3.2.

TABLE 3.1 Four aggregates of gross product

	£ millions at current prices		1978 as % of
	1975	1978	1975
Gross domestic product:			
at factor cost	93502	141999	151·9
at market prices	103949	161639	155·5
Gross national product:			
at factor cost	94264	142835	151·5
at market prices	104711	162475	155·2

SOURCE
1979 *Blue Book*, Table 1.1.

TABLE 3.2 Adjustments between gross product aggregates

	£ million at current prices	
	1975	1978
From domestic to national:		
add net property income from abroad	762	836
From factor cost to market prices		
add indirect taxes	14163	23238
less subsidies	− 3716	− 3598
i.e. add net indirect taxes	10447	19640

SOURCE
Table 3.1.

The percentages of Table 3.1 show that each aggregate rose by a little over 50 per cent from 1975 to 1978 – partly real growth but mainly price inflation. The valuations at market prices rose rather more rapidly than those at factor cost. This is because a large increase in indirect taxes in the period was reinforced by an actual reduction in subsidies. As a result, net indirect taxes were about 90 per cent higher in 1978 than in 1975.

3.3 GDP from the Expenditure Side

Estimates of expenditure on GDP are given for 1975 and 1978 in Table 3.3, both at market prices and at factor cost. The method is that described in 2.5 using formulae (B) and (C) of 2.3 above. In the first column of the table, total domestic expenditure is given in three broad components and adjusted, by adding exports and deducting imports, to get GDP at market prices. Net indirect taxes are split over the components in the second column, giving GDP and its components at factor cost in the third column.

TABLE 3.3 GDP from the expenditure side (in £ millions at current prices)

		At market prices	less net indirect taxes	At factor cost
1975	Consumers' expenditure	63704	− 7953	55751
	Government final consumption	23050	− 799	22251
	Gross domestic capital formation[1]	19068	− 977	18091
	Exports of goods and services	27145[2]	− 718	26427
	less imports of goods and services	− 29018[2]	–	− 29018
	GDP	103949	− 10447	93502
1978	Consumers' expenditure	96086	− 14134	81952
	Government final consumption	32693	− 1729	30964
	Gross domestic capital formation[1]	30746	− 2015	28731
	Exports of goods and services	47636[2]	− 1762	45874
	less imports of goods and services	− 45522[2]	–	− 45522
	GDP	161639	− 19640	141999

NOTES
[1] Including increases in stocks: − 1625 in 1975 and 1327 in 1978 at market prices.
[2] Valued as in balance of payments, i.e. exports include but imports exclude net indirect taxes.
SOURCE
1979 *Blue Book*, Table 1.1.

The treatment of net indirect taxes on imports is to be noticed. At market prices, both exports and imports are valued as in the balance of payments: fob (free on board) for goods and transaction values for services. Export values include net indirect taxes, removed on going to factor cost. On the other hand, imports are valued before net indirect taxes and remain unchanged at factor cost. The implication of this method (2.3 above) is that GDP at market prices is left inclusive of net indirect taxes on imports – a substantial figure, some 35 per cent of all net indirect taxes.

The first three items of Table 3.3 make up total domestic expenditure. Between 1975 and 1978, consumers' expenditure rose by a little over 50 per cent at market prices and by rather less at factor cost. Government spending rose rather more slowly and capital formation more rapidly in the period. As a result, total domestic expenditure, like consumers' expenditure, increased by a little over 50 per cent.

TABLE 3.4 Derivation of expenditure on GDP

	£ millions at current prices		1978 as % of
	1975	1978	1975
Total domestic expenditure at market prices	105822	159525	150·7
plus exports of goods and services*	+27145	+47636	175·5
Total final expenditure at market prices	132967	207161	155·8
less imports of goods and services*	−29018	−45522	156·9
GDP at market prices	103949	161639	155·5
less net indirect taxes	−10447	−19640	187·5
GDP at factor cost	93502	141999	151·9

NOTE
* Valued as in balance of payments.
SOURCE
Table 3.3 above.

Table 3.4 sets out the stages from total domestic expenditure, through two intermediate stops shown in Fig. 2.6 above, to GDP at factor cost. It is a matter of running down the first column of Table 3.3 and of deducting net indirect taxes at the end. Both total final expenditure and GDP at market prices increased more rapidly than total domestic expenditure and also more rapidly than GDP at factor cost. This was because of the higher rate of increase recorded by exports and by net indirect taxes.

3.4 GDP from the Income Side

The income measure of GDP at factor cost is given before and after stock appreciation in Table 1.2 of the *Blue Book*, and further details before stock appreciation in Table 4.1. These data are used to construct Tables 3.5, 3.6 and 3.7 here, designed to show both the make-up of GDP as income and the incidence of stock appreciation.

Table 3.5 gives the main categories of income before stock appreciation in 1975 and 1978, together with some details of the largest category — income from employment. What stands out is that gross trading profits increased at a much faster rate than wages and salaries in this period of recovery. Before attempting an explanation, however, we

TABLE 3.5 GDP from income side, before and after stock appreciation

	£ millions at current prices 1975	1978	1978 as % of 1975
Employment income:			
Wages and salaries	59176	84383	142·6
Pay in cash and kind of HM Forces	1283	1643	128·1
Employers' contributions:			
national insurance	4077	6054	148·5
other[1]	3865	6076	157·2
Total	68401	98156	143·5
Self-employment income	9034	13245	146·6
Rent and imputed rent[2]	6459	9842	152·4
Imputed charges[3]	855	1283	150·1
Gross trading profits	13394	22651	169·1
Total, before stock appreciation	98143	145177	147·9
less stock appreciation	−5529	−4249	
Residual error	888	1071	
GDP at factor cost	93502	141999	151·9

NOTES
[1] Contributions to pension funds, compensation to injured employees and certain redundancy payments.
[2] Rent of all rented properties, imputed rent of owner-occupied dwellings and farms.
[3] For consumption of non-trading capital (owner-occupied property).
SOURCE
1979 *Blue Book*, Tables 1.2 and 4.1.

need to allow for stock appreciation, particularly in view of the fact that it was lower in 1978.

The two categories affected, self-employment income and profits, are shown both before and after stock appreciation in Table 3.6. Estimates of self-employment income in the three components shown in the footnote to the table are too rough to be given after stock appreciation. Gross trading profits, however, are shown before and after stock appreciation for companies, public corporations and government enterprises separately. It is seen that the increase in profits is much higher from 1975 to 1978 when taken after stock appreciation. This is particularly so for the profits of companies.

TABLE 3.6 Self-employment income and gross trading profits

	Before stock appreci- ation	*less stock appreci- ation*	*After stock appreci- ation*
1975 £ million at current prices:			
Self-employment income	9034*	−849	8185
Gross trading profits:			
Companies	10146	−4262	5884
Public corporations	3093	−348	2745
Government enterprises	155	−70	85
1978 £ million at current prices:			
Self-employment income	13245*	−753	12492
Gross trading profits:			
Companies	17055	−3087	13968
Public corporations	5412	−354	5058
Government enterprises	184	−55	129
1978 as % of 1975:			
Self-employment income	146·6		152·6
Gross trading profits:			
Companies	168·1		237·4
Public corporations	175·0		184·3
Government enterprises	118·7		151·8

NOTE
* Made from incomes (in

£ millions) of:	*Farmers*	*Professionals*	*Other sole traders*
1975	1895	1457	5682
1978	2501	2039	8705

SOURCE
1979 *Blue Book*, Tables 1.2 and 4.1.

The main categories of income, appropriately valued after stock appreciation, are assembled in Table 3.7 and the percentage distribution calculated in 1975 and in 1978. The effect of the low increase in employment income and the much faster rise in profits after stock appreciation is clear. The share of labour in the total product fell from some 74 per cent in 1975 to just under 70 per cent in 1978. There was a

TABLE 3.7 Shares in GDP as income

After stock appreciation before residual error	£ millions at current prices		% Share	
	1975	1978	1975	1978
Employment income	68401	98156	73·9	69·6
Self-employment income	8185	12492	8·8	8·9
Rent and imputed charges	7314	11125	7·9	7·9
Gross trading profits	8714	19155	9·4	13·6
GDP at factor cost	92614	140928	100·0	100·0

SOURCE
Tables 3.5 and 3.6 above.

corresponding increase in the share of company and other profits. The share of labour was unusually high and that of profits unusually low in 1975, and for two reasons. One reason is that 1975 was a year of depression and profits were squeezed; the other is that rises in wages and salaries were especially large in 1974 and 1975. The period from 1975 to 1978 was one of economic recovery and of largely effective incomes policies. The result in effect was that the share of employment income returned to the normal and fairly stable figure of rather under 70 per cent.

3.5 Cross-classification by Industry and Type of Income

An allocation of income by industry, in some detail and before stock appreciation, is made in Table 3.1 of the *Blue Book* on the basis of the 1968 Standard Industrial Classification. The only split of income which can be used uniformly over all industries is a very broad one: income from employment as opposed to all other forms of income. Table 1.10 of the *Blue Book* then provides for the deduction of stock appreciation in getting the contribution (value added) to GDP at factor cost of each of thirteen industrial groups into which the economy is divided. This rather

TABLE 3.8 GDP by industry and income type (in £ millions at current prices)

	Employment income	Other income[1]	less stock appreciation	Value added
1975 Agriculture, forestry and fishing	889	2218	−577	2530
Industrial production[2]	29071	12025	−3548	37548
Transport and communication	5875	2210	−21	8064
Distributive trades	6547	4028	−1154	9421
Banking, finance, etc[3]	3771	2960	−	6731
Ownership of dwellings	−	5585	−	5585
Government services[4]	13868	700	−	14568
Other services	8380	3782	−229	11933
Total	68401	33508	−5529	96380
Adjustment for financial services				−3766
Residual error				888
GDP at factor cost				93502
1978 Agriculture, forestry and fishing	1273	2978	−536	3715
Industrial production[2]	41507	19606	−2574	58539
Transport and communication	8115	3584	−11	11688
Distributive trades	9439	6157	−909	14687
Banking, finance, etc.[3]	6067	5201	−	11268
Ownership of dwellings	−	8578	−	8578
Government services[4]	18832	1039	−	19871
Other services	12923	5976	−219	18680
Total	98156	53119	−4249	147026
Adjustment for financial services				−6098
Residual error				1071
GDP at factor cost				141999

NOTES
[1] Self-employment income, rent, imputed charges, gross trading profits.
[2] Mining, quarrying, manufacturing, construction, gas, water, electricity.
[3] Insurance, banking, finance, real estate, business services.
[4] Public administration, defence, public health and education.
SOURCE
1979 *Blue Book*, Tables 1.10 and 3.1.

simple cross-classification is shown here in Table 3.8 for 1975 and 1978. The two-way split of income is shown in the columns. The number of industrial groups in the rows is cut down to eight for ease of comparison.

The share of employment income in total product in 1978 was a fairly normal figure of just under 70 per cent (Table 3.7). Apart from a minor qualification on the duplication of financial services, Table 3.8 shows how this share varies from one industrial group to another. It is far from uniform, as must be expected from the variety of economic activity. At one end of the spectrum, the ownership of dwellings has no labour costs, all income being rent. At the other end, value added by government (non-trading) services is all labour on the treatment adopted (2.3 above), apart from a small imputed charge for owner-occupied non-trading property (2.9 above). The share of employment income is low in agriculture and distribution, industries with much self-employment. The labour share is above average in industrial production, though below average in transport and communication; here there are many labour-intensive as well as some capital-intensive industries.

3.6 GDP from the Output Side

The contributions (value added) of industries to GDP at factor cost in 1975 and 1978 are given in Table 3.9, all thirteen groups identified in Table 1.10 of the *Blue Book* being shown. The percentage increases between the two years include two large ones: for mining and quarrying and for the utilities of gas, electricity and water. The first of these groups includes North Sea oil and gas, which were developing rapidly after 1975.

The changing pattern of industries in the economy is to be seen most clearly in the percentage distributions of Table 3.10, where the same groups of industries are used as in Table 3.8. Since the adjustment for financial services cannot be made in this table, the percentages are somewhat high for industries making much use of financial services and low for others. The groups with increasing shares in total product between 1975 and 1978 were partly within industrial production – North Sea oil and gas, utilities and some manufacturing industries – and partly in service trades such as distribution, banking and finance.

One of the industrial categories of these tables is the important group of *industrial production*, dominated by manufacturing, but also including mining, quarrying, North Sea oil and gas, construction and the utilities. This group accounts for about 40 per cent of all GDP at factor

TABLE 3.9 GDP from output side, after stock appreciation.

	£ millions at current prices 1975	1978	1978 as % of 1975
Agriculture, forestry and fishing	2530	3715	146·8
Mining and quarrying	1475	4467	302·8
Manufacturing	26256	40690	155·0
Construction	6823	8610	126·2
Gas, electricity, water	2994	4772	159·4
Transport	5232	7677	146·7
Communication	2832	4011	141·6
Distributive trades	9421	14687	155·9
Banking, finance, etc	6731	11268	167·4
Ownership of dwellings	5585	8578	153·6
Public administration and defence	7385	10197	138·1
Public health and education	7183	9674	134·7
Other services	11933	18680	156·5
Total	96380	147026	152·5
Adjustment for financial services	−3766	−6098	
Residual error	888	1071	
GDP at factor cost	93502	141999	151·9

SOURCE
1979 *Blue Book*, Table 1.10.

TABLE 3.10 Contributions of industrial groups to GDP

After stock appreciation, before adjustment for financial services, before residual error	% distribution of value added 1975	1978
Agriculture, forestry and fishing	2·6	2·5
Industrial production	39·0	39·8
Transport and communication	8·4	7·9
Distributive trades	9·8	10·0
Banking, finance, etc	7·0	7·7
Ownership of dwellings	5·8	5·8
Government services	15·1	13·5
Other services	12·4	12·7
GDP at factor cost	100·0	100·0

SOURCE
Table 3.9; see notes to Table 3.8 above. Percentages need not add to 100·0 because of rounding.

cost. A large amount of information is published on industrial production, in this sense, much of it in the form of monthly and quarterly statistics.

4 Sector Accounts

4.1 Introduction

Following the lead of 2.4 above, we now consider the economy as divided into sectors and proceed to put together the relevant accounts for each sector. The accounts used for illustration in the present chapter are taken from the run of summary tabulations in the *Blue Book*: Tables 1.3–1.8 inclusive. These can be supplemented by reference to the useful Table 9.1 setting out combined accounts for central and local government.

The four main sectors can be briefly described in the following terms:

1 *Personal Sector*: all individuals, whether in households or not and including those self-employed in unincorporated businesses, together with private non-profitmaking bodies.
2 *Corporate Sector*: companies as privately controlled corporate enterprises, financial institutions of all kinds and public corporations (nationalised industries).
3 *Government*: central government, national insurance funds and local authorities, as trading enterprises and in their non-trading activities.
4 *Overseas Sector*: transactions of UK nationals with foreigners as shown in the UK balance of payments accounts.

Notice that the personal sector includes all the activities of the self-employed. It is not possible in practice to separate, in the accounts of unincorporated enterprises, the owner's personal from his business transactions. On the other hand, the corporate sector includes all financial institutions whether they are incorporated or not. Building societies, for example, are included though not incorporated. Private non-profitmaking bodies such as charities and universities are allocated to the personal sector since there is nowhere else for them to go; certainly they would not fit into the profit-making activities of the corporate sector.

Of the three types of accounts which can be constructed for a sector,

47

the *operating account* makes only an incidental appearance in the *Blue Book* and it will not be pursued here. In setting sales and other revenue against expenses, it throws up gross trading profits or surplus as the balance. It is this balance which is important; it is transferred to the next type of account to consider: the *income and expenditure account*. This is a familiar construct in which incomes or receipts are set against expenditures or allocations. It goes under several titles, e.g. appropriation account for companies, current account for government or the overseas sector. The balance thrown up in the account is the saving of the sector. In effect, the account represents the *ex post* identity of income with expenditure *plus* saving.

The third type of account is the *capital account* which takes over, on its receipts side, the saving balance in the income and expenditure account. Receipts are then set against capital expenditures of all kinds, on real and on financial assets, and without any balance left over. The account reflects the *ex post* identity between saving and investment.

It is in the sector accounts that double-entry book-keeping plays its major role. It is not only that items on one side of a sector account match those on the other side, but also a matter of transferring a credit item in one account to appear again as a debit item in another account. For example, saving as the balance on the debit side of the income and expenditure account of a sector reappears on the credit side of the capital account. Notice how wide is the range of double-entry credits and debits. They are by no means confined to current money transactions; transfers play an important part in balancing the accounts. For example, the income and expenditure account of the personal sector has government grants on one side and taxes paid to government on the other. The same items appear, but switched between the credit and debit sides, in the current account for government. Both items are simply transfers between persons and government.

4.2 Personal Sector

The income and expenditure account of the personal sector has the various components of total personal income on the credit side. The four main categories, as in formula (C) of 2.4 above, are shown for 1975 and 1978 in Table 4.1, together with an additional entry representing imputed charges for capital consumption of non-profitmaking bodies (2.9 above). To get from total personal income to GNP at factor cost requires the exclusion of transfers (current grants and national debt

TABLE 4.1 Personal sector: income and expenditure account

	£ millions at current prices		% share	
	1975	1978	1975	1978
Income from:				
Employment	68401	98156	70·7	68·5
Self-employment[1]	9034	13245	9·3	9·2
Rent, dividends, net interest	8857	13671	9·2	9·5
Current grants[2]	10325	17897	10·7	12·5
Imputed charges[3]	155	244	0·2	0·2
Total personal income	96772	143213	100·0	100·0
Expenditure:				
Consumers' expenditure[4]	55751	81952	57·6	57·2
Net indirect taxes	7953	14134	8·2	9·9
Taxes on income	15077	19672	15·6	13·7
NI contributions	6845	10023	7·1	7·0
Net transfers to abroad	143	218	0·1	0·2
Balance: saving[5]	11003	17214	11·4	12·0
Total	96772	143213	100·0	100·0

NOTES
[1] Before stock appreciation.
[2] National insurance benefits, other current grants from government and current transfers from companies to charities.
[3] For consumption of non-trading capital (owner-occupied property) of non-profit-making bodies.
[4] At factor cost after deduction of net indirect taxes.
[5] Before stock appreciation; including additions to tax reserves (£ 200 million in 1975 and minus £17 million in 1978) and to funds of life assurance companies and of superannuation schemes.
SOURCE
1979 *Blue Book*, Tables 1.1 and 1.3. Percentages need not add to 100·0 because of rounding.

interest) and the addition of certain income attributable to UK nationals but not in personal income. The main item to be added is the undistributed profits of the corporate sector (see 4.3 below).

On the expenditure side of the account, the two main categories are consumers' expenditure and transfers to the government as taxes and as contributions (by employees and employers) to national insurance funds. Consumers' expenditure is estimated at market prices but it can be obtained also at factor cost by the deduction of net indirect taxes (Table 3.3 above). The second alternative is adopted in Table 4.1 since it has the advantage of showing all personal taxation, both direct and indirect, together in one tabulation. One adjustment needs to be made before a balance is struck. Personal transfers to abroad are met partly by transfers to the personal sector from abroad (not in personal income) and partly out of income. It follows that the excess of transfers to abroad over those from abroad is an additional entry on the expenditure side.

The balance in the account appears on the expenditure side and it is to be interpreted as saving by the personal sector. Taxes are shown in the account as those actually paid. It follows that any additions to tax reserves made by the personal sector are included in saving; they are shown in the footnote to Table 4.1. Additions made to life assurance and superannuation funds, considered as the collective property of the members (2.7 above), are also included in saving. This is why the contributions by employees and employers to private pension funds are not shown separately in the account in the same way as contributions to national insurance.

Notice that the income side of Table 4.1 is before deduction of stock appreciation. It follows that saving, the balance on the expenditure side, is also before stock appreciation. Estimates of stock appreciation included in self-employment income are given in Table 3.6 above.

The shares of different forms of personal income are calculated in Table 4.1. Employment income, a little under 70 per cent of GDP in 1978, was much the same proportion of total personal income. Of even more interest is the percentage distribution of total expenditure over the main categories, also calculated in Table 4.1. The main change from 1975 to 1978 was the switch from direct to indirect taxes; saving was

TABLE 4.2 Personal disposable income (in £ millions at current prices)

	1975	1978
Total personal income	96772	143213
less taxes on income, NI contributions and net transfers to abroad	− 22065	− 29913
Personal disposable income	74707	113300
Consumers' expenditure at market prices	63704	96086
Balance: saving	11003	17214
Saving as % of personal disposable income	14·7	15·2

SOURCE:
Table 4.1 above.

some 12 per cent of total income and expenditure in 1978 much as in 1975.

It is more usual to express saving as a proportion not of total personal income, but of disposable income. This is done in Table 4.2, where the proportion is seen to be about 15 per cent in both years. The percentage saved was much lower in the early 1970s and rose sharply in the depression year of 1975.

4.3 Corporate Sector

The income and expenditure of the corporate sector in what is generally known as the appropriation account comprise income from profits and other services and the allocation to dividends, interest and taxation. The balance, on the expenditure or allocation side of the account, is corporate saving in the form of undistributed income. Taxes are actual payments, as in the personal sector, leaving additions to tax reserves to be included in corporate saving. Similarly, dividends and interest are as paid out and additions to dividend and interest reserves are in saving.

Table 4.3 sets out the corporate account for 1975 and 1978. Separate accounts on these lines are published in the *Blue Book* for companies, for financial institutions and for public corporations. Additions to reserves, left in corporate saving, are shown in a footnote to Table 4.3. Notice that these additions can be negative, as for tax reserves in 1975, indicating a net reduction in the reserves during a year.

Gross trading profits make up some 60 per cent of corporate income; it was a little higher in 1978 after a period of recovery. On the other hand, because of continuing restrictions on dividend payments between 1975 and 1978, a falling proportion of corporate income was paid out as dividends and interest. As a result, after allowance for more paid abroad and to the taxman, the level of corporate saving was proportionately higher in 1978.

4.4 Government

The current (income and expenditure) account of the government sector can be shown for central and for local government separately, as in Tables 1.5 and 1.6 of the *Blue Book*, or it can be arranged in a combined form for the whole sector with the aid of Table 9.1 of the *Blue Book*. The combined account is the one summarised here, in Table 4.4, for 1975 and 1978.

TABLE 4.3 Corporate sector: appropriation account

	£ millions at current prices		% share	
	1975	1978	1975	1978
Income				
Gross trading profits[1]	13239	22467	61·0	63·6
Rent and non-trading income	6081	8825	28·0	25·0
Income form abroad[2]	2370	4043	10·9	11·4
Total	21690	35335	100·0	100·0
Expenditure				
Dividends and interest paid	8086	10558	37·3	29·9
Current transfers to charities	42	44	0·2	0·1
Profits due abroad[3]	627	2002	2·9	5·7
Taxes on income	2297	3807	10·6	10·8
Balance: saving[4]	10638	18924	49·0	53·6
Total	21690	35335	100·0	100·0

NOTES

[1] Before stock appreciation.
[2] Net of local taxes and before stock appreciation.
[3] Net of UK taxes.
[4] Undistributed income after tax and before stock appreciation.

Includings (in £ millions) additions to:	1975	1978
tax reserves	− 337	1354
dividend and interest reserves	189	318

SOURCE

1979 *Blue Book*, Table 1.4. Percentages need not add to 100·0 because of rounding.

Direct and indirect taxes are the bulk (about 73 per cent) of government income and national insurance contributions account for another 16 per cent. The latter, for the most part, go into the National Insurance Fund, sometimes shown separately and sometimes with central government. Trading profits, rents of council housing and interest on loans to public corporations make up well under 10 per cent of all income. Apart from the switch from direct to indirect taxes already noted, the proportions of the sources of income are fairly stable over time.

Over half the spending of central and local government is on what has been called (in 2.2 above) the final consumption of government: wages,

TABLE 4.4 Government: combined current account

| | £ millions at current prices | | % share | |
	1975	1978	1975	1978
Income				
Gross trading surplus[1]	155	184	0·4	0·3
Rent, dividends, interest	3580	5159	8·5	8·3
Indirect taxes[2]	14163	23238	33·7	37·5
Taxes on income	16632	22321	39·5	36·0
NI contributions	6845	10023	16·3	16·2
Imputed charges[3]	700	1039	1·7	1·7
Total income	42075	61964	100·0	100·0
Expenditure				
Final consumption	23050	32693	54·8	52·8
Subsidies	3716	3598	8·8	5·8
Current grants				
to persons	10283	17853	24·4	28·8
paid abroad[4]	367	1700	0·9	2·7
Debt interest	4212	7302	10·0	11·8
Balance: saving[5]	447	−1182	1·1	−1·9
Total expenditure	42075	61964	100·0	100·0

NOTES
[1] Before stock appreciation.
[2] Taxes on expenditure including rates, before deduction of subsidies.
[3] For consumption of non-trading capital (owner-occupied property).
[4] Grants, subscriptions and contributions to international organisations *less* transfers from EEC.
[5] Before stock appreciation. Made up (in £ millions) from saving by:

	1975	1978
central government	−714	−2914
local authorities	1161	1732

SOURCE
1979 *Blue Book*, Tables 1.5, 1.6 and 9.1. Percentages need not add to 100·0 because of rounding.

salaries and a variety of current purchases. Of the rest, two items increased their shares between 1975 and 1978: current grants to persons and debt interest. Against this there was a reduced payment of subsidies (3.2 above).

The balance on the expenditure side is the contribution of government to the total saving in the economy. It is not generally a large proportion of the total and in some years it is negative (dis-saving). In 1978, dis-saving by central government more than offset the normal saving by local authorities.

4.5 Summary Capital Account

Each sector has its own capital account but what is shown here, in Table 4.5, is a condensed summary of the combined account for all sectors. The form is simple, a representation of the identity between saving and investment. Receipts are the savings of sectors, brought down from the balances in Tables 4.1, 4.3 and 4.4. Payments are investments in fixed assets and stocks in the domestic economy together with net investment abroad.

There are several ways of presenting the account. Saving on the receipts side can be given before or after depreciation. Table 4.5 opts for showing all values gross, without deduction of depreciation. On the

TABLE 4.5 Summary capital account (in £ millions at current prices)

	1975		1978	
Receipts				
Total saving[1]		22088		34956
Personal sector	11003		17214	
Corporate sector	10638		18924	
Government	447		−1182	
less stock appreciation		−5529		−4249
Residual error		888		1071
Total		17447		31778
Payments				
Total gross domestic fixed capital formation		20545		29218
Personal sector	3122		5525	
Corporate sector	12449		19307	
Government	4974		4386	
Total increase in stocks[2]		−1477		1528
Personal sector	−326		216	
Corporate sector	−1172		1230	
Government	21		82	
Net investment abroad[3]		−1621		1032
Total		17447		31778

NOTES
[1] Before stock appreciation; including additions to tax, dividend and interest reserves.
[2] Value of physical increase in stocks and work in progress.
[3] Balance of current account, including current transfers, in the UK balance of payments (5.6 below).
SOURCE
1979 *Blue Book*, Table 1.8.

other hand, saving is given after deduction of stock appreciation, taken off in a single figure at the bottom. This means that, on the payments side, domestic fixed capital formation is gross and the stocks entry is the value of the physical increase, deducting stock appreciation from the increase in book values.

One further adjustment is needed in Table 4.5. The estimates of saving come from the income side in the national accounts and those of investment from the expenditure side. The residual error (2.5 above) is needed to achieve a balance, shown (as usual in the UK accounts) on the income side.

The figures of saving and investment by sectors are very variable from one year to another and it is not appropriate to calculate either percentage changes or percentage distributions in Table 4.5. The main investments are made by the corporate and government sectors; those in the personal sector are largely dwellings, together with some purchases of plant and equipment by the self-employed. On the other hand, a large proportion of total saving is by the personal sector, leaving funds available for investment elsewhere and particularly by central government and local authorities. The most variable form of investment is that in stocks. In most years, as in the recovery to 1978, stocks are built up, sometimes slowly and sometimes more rapidly. In a few years, as in the depression year of 1975, stocks were reduced, a form of dis-investment.

5 Balance of Payments

5.1 Introduction

The accounts of the overseas sector remain to be considered. The current account is presented here in some detail and the capital account in summary form. Between them they make up the complete balance of payments of the UK, credits and debits exactly offsetting each other.

The current account is of standard income/expenditure form constructed from the totality of current international transactions of the UK. Exports of goods and services together with property income received from abroad go on the credit side; debits are the corresponding imports of goods and services and property income paid abroad. As for all sector accounts (4.1 above) the current account includes transfers (here from and to abroad) before a balance is struck. The balance in the current account of the overseas sector is to be interpreted as the net funds available for investment abroad. Finally the current account balance, as net investment abroad, is carried forward to the capital account and appears as the excess of capital outflows over capital inflows.

As has already been mentioned, complete data on the balance of payments year by year are published in the *Pink Book* and quarterly figures in rather less detail in articles in *Economic Trends* in March, June, September and December. A condensed version of the current account is published in the *Blue Book* and in the quarterly articles on national income and expenditure in *Economic Trends*.

There is, however, one minor discrepancy. The United Kingdom of the balance of payments is Great Britain, Northern Ireland, the UK part of the North Sea oil and gas fields, the Channel Islands and the Isle of Man. The national income accounts, however, take the UK as excluding the Channel Islands and the Isle of Man. In a transfer of data from the balance of payments to the national accounts, therefore, exports of Great Britain and Northern Ireland to the islands should be added to exports, and exports from the islands to the rest of the world deducted. A similar adjustment should be made for imports. No such adjustments are made in practice. There remains a discrepancy, one which is so small that it is not worth the cost of correction.

A detailed account of how the current account of the balance of payments is taken over into the national income accounts is in *Source and Methods*, at pp. 436–67. The *Pink Book* is divided into sections each of which starts, conveniently, with technical notes, and it ends with a glossary of terms and a section on exchange rates. The latter says: 'When information is recorded in currencies other than sterling, the figures are as far as possible converted into sterling at the rate of exchange at the time of the transaction (1979 *Pink Book*, p. 92).

5.2. Visible Trade

The current account of the UK balance of payments is split into two types of transactions: visibles and invisibles. This is convenient since current statistics on visibles – trade in goods as opposed to services – are available more frequently and in more detail than those on other current items lumped together as invisibles. The basic data on trade in goods is published monthly by the Department of Trade in *Overseas Trade Statistics*. When transferred to the balance of payments, and then to the national income accounts, these data need adjustment to match the concepts of the national accounts.

Table 5.1 shows the adjustments, starting from the overseas trade statistics and ending with the figures on a balance of payments basis. The former are built up from returns from exporters and importers on methods devised for the purpose by H.M. Customs. The adjustments are of three kinds: corrections for the underrecording of exports; an amended set of valuations; adjustments for coverage. The first arise since it was discovered that, around 1969 and at intervals since, exports were not completely recorded or fully valued in the returns from exporters. (A similar discrepancy does not occur for importers' returns, which are more carefully scrutinised by H.M. Customs with their eyes on their obligation to levy import duties). Methods were devised to eliminate the underrecording or (when not fully eliminated) to correct for it.

The main valuation adjustment is to reduce the cif (cost, insurance, freight) values returned by importers to the fob (free on board) values used for exports. The insurance and freight charges are switched to the appropriate entries under services amongst invisibles (Table 5.2 below). Another valuation adjustment is the elimination of 'customs uplift'

TABLE 5.1 Visible trade (in £ millions at current prices)

	Exports		Imports	
Adjustments	*1975*	*1978*	*1975*	*1978*
Overseas Trade Statistics[1]	20198	37363	24431	40969
Under-recording of exports	–	+ 112	–	–
Valuation:				
Freight and insurance	–	–	– 1415	– 1963
Other	–	–	– 63	– 239
Coverage:				
Secondhand ships	+ 149	+ 175	+ 56	+ 22
Secondhand aircraft	– 133	– 389	– 137	– 453
Ships delivered abroad	–	–	+ 440	+ 346
No change in ownership	– 711	– 1739	– 690	– 1714
Other	– 40	– 90	+ 77	– 361
Balance of payments[2]	19463	35432	22699	36607

NOTES
[1] Exports fob, imports cif.
[2] Exports and imports fob.
SOURCE
1979 *Pink Book*, Table 2.1.

whereby certain imports are valued at open-market prices in excess of those actually paid.

Coverage adjustments are for those items which should be but are not in the overseas trade statistics, and for those which are but should not be in these statistics. Secondhand ships bought or sold abroad and new ships (and drilling rigs) delivered abroad to British owners are in the first category. The second includes secondhand aircraft which are not sold but sent abroad, or brought into the UK, for repair. There is also, in the second category, a great variety of returned goods as well as those sent out or brought in for repairs with no change in ownership.

The adjustments of Table 5.1 are condensed from details given in the *Pink Book* and relate to annual data. They are made, however, on a continuing basis, by the Department of Trade, month by month. The monthly figures in (e.g.) the *Monthly Digest of Statistics* are on a balance of payments basis as well as in the original form from exporters' and importers' returns.

5.3 Invisibles: Trade in Services

International transactions include current services of many types and the sources of information on them are more diversified and less reliable and timely than for trade in goods. Table 5.2 shows the main categories in 1975 and 1978. The credits here are exports of services to match exports of goods and the debits are the corresponding imports of services.

TABLE 5.2 Trade in services (in £ millions at current prices)

	1975			1978		
	Credits	Debits	Balance	Credits	Debits	Balance
Private:*						
Sea transport	2634	2603	+31	3163	3334	−171
Civil aviation	780	664	+116	1448	1100	+348
Travel	1218	917	+301	2503	1548	+955
Financial	1005	–	+1005	1488	–	+1488
Other	1906	1426	+480	3284	1918	+1366
Total private	7543	5610	+1933	11886	7900	+3986
Total government	139	709	−570	318	1015	−697

NOTE
* Including public corporations.
SOURCE
1979 *Pink Book*, Table 1.2.

Sea transport and civil aviation are two services with large credits and debits but relatively small balances. The balance on civil aviation is a net credit and one which has increased in the 1970s. The balance on sea transport is a small net credit in some years (e.g. 1975) but more usually a net debit as in 1978. Neither item represents the total earnings of British operators since much of the revenue comes from UK nationals with no charge to the balance of payments. The credits are: freight on exports and on cross-trade, charter receipts and passenger revenue from foreigners by UK operators, *plus* disbursements in the UK by foreign operators. Similarly the debits are: freight on imports and the revenue from British passengers carried by foreign operators, *plus* charter payments and disbursements overseas by UK operators. The data, given in Tables 3.3 to 3.6 of the 1979 *Pink Book*, came from returns from the General Council of British Shipping, British Airways and the British independent airlines, together with a variety of sources on the operations of foreign shipping and airlines.

Travel is another large item, both on the credit and on the debit side, and it has shown an increasing net credit balance since the early 1970s.

Credits are expenditures on goods, internal transport and other services by overseas visitors in the UK and debits are the corresponding expenses overseas by UK tourists. The cost of transport to and from the UK is in the previous two items, not in this one. The travel is for business, for holidays and for such purposes as student travel, visits to friends and relatives and sporting events. The estimates are obtained mainly from a continuing survey conducted by the Department of Trade: the International Passenger Survey.

Financial services are the net earnings from overseas of financial institutions in the UK: insurance, banking, brokerage, merchanting and, as a recent addition, overseas work done by solicitors. Corresponding earnings by foreign financial concerns are negligible and no debit entry is raised.

The miscellaneous services called 'other' in Table 5.2 are even more varied. Examples are: films, TV and other royalties; fees from overseas students; agencies, advertising and management consultants; commissions on trade in goods; services related to the oil and gas operators in the British sector of the North Sea.

The sources of data on the last two categories include such returns as those from: the Bank of England; Lloyds and the British Insurance Association; the British Council for overseas students; VAT for solicitors' earnings; the British Export Houses Association for merchanting; Department of Trade enquiries on royalties. Net earnings derived from financial and other services overseas have been and still are very large.

On the other hand, government services produce a substantial debit balance. The credits come mainly from expenditures by foreign military forces and by EEC institutions in the UK. The debits are the larger expenditures overseas by H.M. Government on military, diplomatic and other operations. The earnings of public corporations from their services overseas are not here but in the private sector.

5.4 Invisibles: Property Income and Transfers

These are the remaining two categories in the current account of the balance of payments. Estimates for 1975 and 1978 are summarised in Table 5.3, in which each of the two categories is split into receipts and payments by the private sector and by government. More detail of property income, for the combined private and government sectors, is given in Table 5.4. In both tables, credits are earnings or receipts from

TABLE 5.3 Property income and transfers (in £ millions at current prices)

	Credits	*1975* Debits	Balance	Credits	*1978* Debits	Balance
Private:[1]						
Property income[2]	2570	1294	+1276	4281	2989	+1292
Transfers	360	503	−143	630	848	−218
Government:						
Property income[2]	266	780	−514	766	1222	−456
Transfers	363	730	−367	454	2154	−1700

NOTES
[1] Including public corporations.
[2] Interest, profits and dividends.
SOURCE
1979 *Pink Book*, Table 1.2.

TABLE 5.4 Property income: detail (in £ millions at current prices)

Income from	1975	1978
Credits:		
Direct investment	1583	2433
Portfolio investment	243	288
Export credits	206	369
Earnings of UK banks[1]	297	526
Other[2]	507	1431
Total	2836	5047
Debits:		
Direct investment	620	1445
Portfolio investment	288	618
Interest on:		
sterling balances	651	511
foreign currency borrowing[3]	212	317
overseas borrowing[4]	167	480
Other[2]	136	840
Total	2074	4211

NOTES
[1] On lending in sterling (to non-residents) and in overseas currencies.
[2] Including operations of oil companies.
[3] On loans by HM Government and by UK public sector under exchange cover scheme.
[4] On loans by local authorities, public corporations and private sector from banks etc overseas.
SOURCE
1979 *Pink Book*, Table 5.1.

abroad by UK nationals and debits are the corresponding payments from the UK domestic economy to foreigners.

Transfers from and to abroad need little said about them. On private account, they include such items as gifts, legacies and migrants' remittances; there is a negative balance, transfers to abroad as debits exceeding transfers from abroad as credits. There is a net debit balance also for government transfers but it is larger and increasing. Large debit items here include economic grants, subscriptions and contributions to international organisations and, more recently, contributions to the EEC.

Property income is the term used in the national income accounts of the *Blue Book* and generally adopted here to maintain continuity with earlier chapters. The same item is called *interest, profits and dividends* in the balance of payments statistics and this may well be more descriptive of the wide range of receipts and payments made across the exchanges in this category of invisibles. On the credit side, the earnings or receipts of UK nationals from overseas, as indicated in Table 5.4, come from such sources as: profits, whether distributed or retained, from subsidiaries and other direct investments abroad; dividends from UK holdings of stocks and shares of foreign companies and governments; interest on loans by British banks to foreigners. All these are taken net of local taxes. On the debit side, the payments are those made to foreigners on their various investments in the UK, (whether direct, portfolio or other) again net of UK tax.

The private sector, again including public corporations, has an excess of property income from abroad over that paid abroad. This net credit, though still large, has been generally decreasing since the early 1970s at current prices as well as in real terms. The income of UK nationals from overseas, particularly from direct investments, remains substantial. What has caused the unfavourable trend is the increase in payments made on overseas investment in the UK. One factor, though not the only one, is the increasing participation of foreign interests in oil and gas drilling in the British sector of the North Sea.

The balance of payments falls the other way for the government sector. Interest on inter-government loans and some other items appear on both sides. The net deficit arises largely because of such large debit items as interest paid on overseas holdings of Treasury Bills and government stocks and on overseas borrowing by the central authorities and, more recently, by local government.

Estimates of property income and transfers from and to abroad come from a number of official returns: from government departments and the Bank of England, from the Inland Revenue and Exchange Control, and from special enquiries, e.g. that on direct investment overseas undertaken by the Department of Industry.

5.5 Balance of Invisibles

Table 5.5 is obtained by assembling the net credit or debit balances for all invisibles in the current account of the balance of payments. The overall balance of invisibles is found to be a considerable net credit. It is, however, the result of a large net credit arising in the private sector, including public corporations, partly offset by the net debit on government transactions.

TABLE 5.5 Balance of invisibles (in £ millions at current prices)

Net credit (+) or debit (−)	1975	1978
Private:		
Services*	+ 1933	+ 3986
Property income*	+ 1276	+ 1292
Transfers	− 143	− 218
Total	+ 3066	+ 5060
Government:		
Services	− 570	− 697
Property income	− 514	− 456
Transfers	− 367	− 1700
Total	− 1451	− 2853
Total invisibles	+ 1615	+ 2207

NOTE
*Including public corporations.
SOURCE
Tables 5.2 and 5.3 above.

Though the overall balance has remained a net credit, the actual figure at current prices has fluctuated widely since the early 1970s. It fell from 1974 to 1975 and then rose sharply in 1976 before falling again to 1977. The net credit in 1978 was 80 per cent of that achieved in 1976 at current prices and an even smaller proportion in real terms.

The two largest factors at work in recent years have been the reduction in net earnings by the private sector from interest, profits and dividends and the increase in official transfers to abroad. The balance of trade in services, at current prices, also levelled off in the private sector in 1978. Part of this adverse change was due to the expanding share of overseas concerns in services rendered to the operators of the North Sea oil and gas fields.

5.6 Balance of Payments: Drawing the Line

This chapter can be appropriately rounded off with a brief description of the complete balance of payments of the UK on current and capital account. The object is not to present the details of current and capital transactions, fascinating though these are. The technical notes in the *Pink Book* give full descriptions of the transactions, and particularly those on capital account. The aim, rather, is to paint a general picture to serve as the backdrop to the stage on which various overseas transactions make their appearances in the national accounts statistics. There are two such appearances.

The first is in the adjustment of total domestic expenditure to GDP from the expenditure side and then to GNP: the addition of exports of goods and services, the deduction of the corresponding imports and the final addition of net property income from abroad. These are just the concepts already discussed in this chapter. The second appearance is that of net investment abroad both in the concept of gross national expenditure, given by formula (G) of 2.2 above, and in the summary capital account of Table 4.5 above.

Table 5.6 displays the general outline of the complete balance of payments. The first entries are for trade in goods, giving a net debit balance marked A in the table. These are valued fob (free on board) as adjusted from the returns published in *Overseas Trade Statistics* (Table 5.1 above). The second entries, with a net credit balance B, are for the corresponding trade in services summarised in Table 5.2. The credits are here described as exports and the debits as imports of services. The current account is completed by bringing in the third entries with a balance C which is a net credit in 1975 and a net debit in 1978. These are the remaining invisibles, property income and transfers from and to abroad; they are here given net, from Table 5.3.

There is little difficulty in interpreting the + and − signs attached to the entries in the current account. Credits + are receipts from overseas by UK nationals; debits − on the corresponding payments made to foreigners.

TABLE 5.6 Balance of payments: complete account (in £ millions at current prices)

	Net credit (+) or debit (−)	
	1975	1978
Exports of goods (fob)	+ 19463	+ 35432
Imports of goods (fob)	− 22699	− 36607
A: Balance, trade in goods	− 3236	− 1175
Exports of services	+ 7682	+ 12204
Imports of services	− 6319	− 8915
B: Balance, trade in services	+ 1363	+ 3289
Property income (net)	+ 762	+ 836
Transfers (net)	− 510	− 1918
C: Balance, other invisibles	+ 252	− 1082
Investment (net):		
in UK	+ 1742	+ 2689
by UK	− 1290	− 4087
Other capital flows (net)	− 326	− 1533
D: Balance, investment, etc.	+ 126	− 2931
E: Balancing item	+ 30	+ 773
Official financing:		
IMF, etc.	−	− 1016
Foreign currency borrowing[1]	+ 810	− 187
Drawing on reserves[2]	+ 655	+ 2329

NOTES
[1] Loans (+) or repayments (−) by HM Government and by UK public sector under exchange cover scheme.
[2] Drawings from (+) or additions to reserves (−).
SOURCE:
1979 *Pink Book*, Tables 1.2 and 1.3.

The next step is the critical one. It is the step indicated at the outset (in 5.1 above); it takes the current account balance, interpreted as the net funds available for investment abroad, and identifies the capital outflows and inflows which balance out to net investment abroad. The fourth set of entries, with balance D in Table 5.6, summarise the capital flows which are concerned with economic activity. Direct and portfolio investments made by foreigners in the private and public sectors of the UK economy are shown first. Similar investments made overseas by UK nationals on private account are the second entry. The third item pulls together all the other capital flows of an economic nature; examples are increases in sterling balances held by overseas governments and other foreigners, and such short-term flows as import and export credits. Official long-term capital movements are also in this entry.

What remains to complete Table 5.6 is the inclusion at the end of entries for official financing. These are the capital flows made by government which are not part of economic activity but are designed to balance the books. The first two entries represent official borrowing, and the corresponding repayments, either from the IMF and other international monetary authorities or directly in foreign currencies. The third entry, the financing of last resort, consists of drawings made from or of additions to the reserves of gold and foreign currencies.

It is important to see how the property income of Table 5.4 is related to the investment and financing items of Table 5.6. Consider property income received from abroad and UK investment overseas; similar comments can be made for flows in the other direction. The basic concept is the *stock* of overseas assets, net of liabilities, held by the private and public sectors of the UK. The *Pink Book* contains much information on these external assets and liabilities. We are not concerned with them here as such, but only with the two flows which are related to them. One flow consists of the interest, profits and dividends obtained in a given year from the overseas assets and this goes into Table 5.4. The other flow is the net additions made to the overseas assets in a given year; these are the investments of Table 5.6.

Particular attention needs to be paid to the + and − signs attached to investment entries. As in the current account, credits + represent receipts or inward flows of funds across the exchanges and debits − are corresponding funds paid out. In the capital account, credits + therefore arise from overseas investment in the UK or from the sale of UK assets overseas; debits − come from UK investment abroad or from the sale of foreign assets in the UK. The temptation must be resisted to consider UK investment abroad as 'good' and so a positive item; it has a negative sign since the funds flow outwards. Other cases to note are: an increase in sterling balances held by foreigners is a + entry; an addition to the reserves is a − entry, since it corresponds to an investment by the UK in an overseas asset (the reserves).

The complete account of the balance of payments is a matter of double-entry book-keeping. Each transaction gives rise to a + entry and to an equal −entry. A hypothetical example serves to illustrate. Suppose that a British group charters an aircraft from Air France for a series of flights and pays the price of £50,000 in sterling, which Air France puts into its sterling balance in London. Result: debit £50,000 in imports of services and credit £50,000 to other capital flows as an increase in sterling balances. Now suppose Air France spends £10,000 on improving its London offices and buys £40,000 worth of dollars to meet fuel bills, both out of its sterling balance. Result: debit £50,000 for a decrease in sterling balances, credit £10,000 for investment in the UK and credit £40,000 for a drawing on the dollar reserves.

It follows that each column of Table 5.6 must add to zero, + entries cancelling − entries on the double-entry system. This is in fact what happens in practice – apart from the usual problem of statistical errors in the estimation process. The accounts of Table 5.6 are balanced off by the inclusion of the *balancing item* shown at E. The item is placed above the official financing entries, and below all the others. This is because official financing is a matter of record, with no errors of estimation, while statistical errors can and do appear in all the other entries in the account.

It also follows that the main interest in the complete account lies in the fact that, when a line is drawn across it at an appropriate place, the sum of the items above the line is exactly equal in magnitude but opposite in sign to the sum of the items below the line. The art consists of knowing where to draw the line; see Paul Allin, 'Drawing the Line in the Balance of Payments Accounts', *Statistical News*, February 1977.

Table 5.7 shows the results of drawing the line in four different places. The first line is drawn immediately below the visibles, the trade in goods.

TABLE 5.7 Balance of payments: drawing the line (in £ million at current prices)

| | | Net credit (+) or debit (−) balance | |
		1975	1978
Trade in goods	A	− 3236	− 1175
Trade in goods and services	A + B	− 1873	+ 2114
Current account	A + B + C	− 1621	+ 1032
For official financing	A + B + C + D + E	− 1465	− 1126
Official financing:			
Borrowing (+) or repayment (−)		+ 810	− 1203
Drawing on reserves (+)		+ 655	+ 2329

SOURCE:
Table 5.6, above.

The balance above the line is the deficit on visible trade, £1175 million in 1978. This is matched by a net credit of the same amount below the line. It is natural to draw the line in this place since the information most readily and frequently available is that on merchandise trade. Drawing the line, however, tells us very little, just that all the other items together – the invisibles, investment and other capital flows, official financing – produce an offsetting net credit of the right amount.

The second line is drawn so that trade in goods and services lies above it while other invisibles and all capital items are below. This line may be suggested by the fact that the net credit on trade in goods and services of some £2100 million in 1978 is used to raise total domestic expenditure to GDP in the national income accounts. As with the first line, and for the same reason, this drawing of the line throws little light on the balance of payments.

The third line is more useful and one commonly drawn. It separates the current account, with a net credit of about £1000 million in 1978, from the capital account below the line. The funds available for investment abroad are this surplus thrown up in the current account and the actual net investment abroad of this amount is identified in the capital account in the bottom half of Table 5.6.

In the event, in 1978 the outflow of funds on direct and portfolio investment overseas by the UK (net of the corresponding investment by foreigners in the UK), together with a variety of short-term capital outflows, was greatly in excess of the net total of investment abroad made possible by current trading. A good deal of dis-investment through drawing on reserves was needed to keep net investment abroad down to the level (about £1000 million) of the current account surplus.

The last line drawn across the account in Table 5.7 is deisgned to show up such features. All current and capital transactions of an economic nature – including the balancing item to allow for errors of estimation – appear above the line. Left below the line is the official financing needed to balance the books.

There was, in 1975 and again in 1978, a large net debit arising from the totality of economic transactions on current and capital account. In 1975 the debit was offset by official borrowing combined with a modest drawing on reserves. In contrast the drawing on reserves was much larger in 1978. It was needed to do two things: first to make the repayment of £1203 million of previous official borrowing (mainly from the IMF) and then to leave enough to offset the deficit of some £1100 million on current and capital transactions of an economic nature.

6 Index Numbers of Quantity and Price

6.1 Introduction

So far the valuation of national income and its components has been at current prices, at the factor cost or market prices of the year considered. The problem now to be tackled is to determine how much of a change in current value arises because of price movements and how much is a real or quantitative change. The question might be put: how much of a recorded change in consumers' expenditure is due to inflation and what is the change in expenditure in real terms?

Values at current prices can be built up from, or equally split down into, the various components without need of more than arithmetical skills of addition and subtraction. This is not so in the present problem: neither quantities nor prices can be added and subtracted. Pints of milk, pounds of butter and numbers of eggs are different and non-additive units. Even if quantities can be expressed in some common unit such as a tonne, as in the example of 6.5 below, it makes no statistical sense to add a tonne of milk to a tonne of butter or eggs. It could make a glorious omelette but not a measure of the output of dairy produce.

The difficulty is overcome by the technique of constructing an index number to measure, not prices or quantities in one year, but the movement from one year to another. What is done is to split the change in a value at current prices into the constituent changes in price and quantity. The changes are shown as percentages and the split is by multiplication rather than by addition. For example, a rise of 15.5 per cent by value may arise from an increase of 5 per cent in quantity combined with a price rise of 10 per cent, as represented by the equation: $1·155 = 1·05 \times 1·10$. Not all changes are increases but there is no arithmetical difficulty. So a situation in which a decrease of 15 per cent in quantity and an increase of 10 per cent in price combine to give a decrease of 6·5 per cent in value is represented as $0·935 = 0·85 \times 1·10$.

The value changes in these examples, even if they are for very heterogeneous aggregates, are arrived at by simple division. If consumers' expenditure, for example, increases from £73·6 million in year 0 to £85 million in year t, then:

Value in year $t = \dfrac{85 \cdot 0}{73 \cdot 6} \times 100 = 115 \cdot 5$ per cent of year 0

or:

Increase in value from years 0 to $t = \dfrac{11 \cdot 4}{73 \cdot 6} \times 100 = 15 \cdot 5$ per cent of year 0

The same trick cannot be turned for changes in price or quantity. A change such as 115·5 per cent is not to be obtained by dividing a sum of prices in year t by the corresponding sum in year 0; it is the result of the calculation of a price index number. Further, such a result is not the unique computation it is with current values. Given a set of data, there are various types of index numbers giving various answers. They are all valid answers; but some may be more appropriate than others in any specific problem. This is familiar enough in statistics. There is (e.g.) no unique average of a set of figures; there is a choice from the arithmetic mean, the geometric mean, the median, and other forms of average.

For an analysis of changing national income there are available certain standard types of index numbers of price and quantity. They can be expressed equivalently as ratios of specified value aggregates and as weighted averages. They are shown formally in a standard shorthand notation in Table 6.1 and developed below.

The notation is as follows. A single item of the aggregate considered has prices p_0 and p_t in years 0 and t; the corresponding quantities are q_0 and q_t. Σ indicates summation over all items; so $\Sigma p_0 q_t$ is the sum got by valuing the quantities of items in year t at the prices of year 0. In particular, the value change from year 0 to year t is $\Sigma p_t q_t$ divided by $\Sigma p_0 q_0$, written V_{0t}. The shorthand symbols used for index numbers are designed to show the types at a glance. Quantity index numbers are shown by Q, those of price by P. The years compared are shown by the subscripts $0t$. The prices or quantities held constant are given in brackets. So $Q_{0t}(p_0)$ indicates a quantity index comparing year t with a base year 0 and got by holding base prices constant.

The notation is chosen so that runs of index numbers can be easily handled. All that is needed is to keep year 0 fixed and to allow year t to vary. The run may be forwards from the base year: $t = 1, 2, 3, \ldots$ It

TABLE 6.1 Index numbers in year t on year 0 as base

Type	Symbol	Definition as ratio of aggregates	Equivalent form as weighted average[1]	Implied form[2]
Laspeyres: Quantity	(1) $Q_{0t}(p_0)$	(1.1) $\dfrac{\Sigma p_0 q_t}{\Sigma p_0 q_0}$	(1.2) $\dfrac{\Sigma w_0 \dfrac{q_t}{q_0}}{\Sigma w_0}$	
Price	(2) $P_{0t}(q_0)$	(2.1) $\dfrac{\Sigma p_t q_0}{\Sigma p_0 q_0}$	(2.2) $\dfrac{\Sigma w_0 \dfrac{p_t}{p_0}}{\Sigma w_0}$	
Paasche: Quantity	(3) $Q_{0t}(p_t)$	(3.1) $\dfrac{\Sigma p_t q_t}{\Sigma p_t q_0}$	(3.2) $\dfrac{\Sigma w_t}{\Sigma w_t \dfrac{q_0}{q_t}}$	(3.3) $\dfrac{V_{0t}}{P_{0t}(q_0)}$
Price	(4) $P_{0t}(q_t)$	(4.1) $\dfrac{\Sigma p_t q_t}{\Sigma p_0 q_t}$	(4.2) $\dfrac{\Sigma w_t}{\Sigma w_t \dfrac{p_0}{p_t}}$	(4.3) $\dfrac{V_{0t}}{Q_{0t}(p_0)}$

(Handwritten marginal notes:) $\dfrac{1}{\Sigma p_0 q_0}\Sigma p_0 q_0\left(\dfrac{q_t}{q_0}\right)$; $\Sigma p_t q_t \dfrac{1}{\Sigma p_t q_t}\left(\dfrac{q_t}{p_0}\right)$

NOTES
[1] Weights $w_0 = p_0 q_0$ or $w_t = p_t q_t$.

[2] As deflation of value change $V_{0t} = \dfrac{\Sigma p_t q_t}{\Sigma p_0 q_0}$.

can, however, go backwards as well as forwards: $t = \ldots -3, -2, -1, 0, 1, 2, 3, \ldots$

6.2 Laspeyres Form

The quantity index of Laspeyres or base-weighted form is (1) of Table 6.1. Its label $Q_{0t}(p_0)$ indicates that it is obtained from values in which the base prices are held constant. The definition (1.1) is: the ratio of the aggregate in question valued in year t at constant (year 0) prices to the aggregate in year 0. It measures the changing cost of the quantities, as they vary over time, at a fixed set of prices, those of the base year. The Laspeyres quantity index has the big advantage that it can be shown in two equivalent ways, simply by switching the units. One way is to take

(1.1), multiply by 100 and write the index $Q_{0t}(p_0)$ with year 0 as 100. The other way is to take the numerator of (1.1) by itself: $\Sigma p_0 q_t$ in £ million. This is simply the aggregate value at constant (year 0) prices. It changes in proportion to $Q_{0t}(p_0)$ since the denominator of $Q_{0t}(p_0)$ is the base year value, a constant independent of t. Only the units are different: $Q_{0t}(p_0)$ in terms of the base value as 100, $\Sigma p_0 q_t$ in £ million. So:

The *Laspeyres quantity index* can be written *either* as $\Sigma p_0 q_t$, the aggregate value in £ million at constant (year 0) prices, *or* as $\dfrac{\Sigma p_0 q_t}{\Sigma p_0 q_0}$ 100 with year 0 as 100. To get the second from the first: divide by the base value ($\Sigma p_0 q_0$) and multiply by 100.

The Laspeyres form has two properties, each a great advantage in practice. The first property is that the real or quantity measure, $\Sigma p_0 q_t$ at constant prices, is the sum of separate components each of the same form. Just as current values add to the total $\Sigma p_t q_t$, so values at constant prices add to the total $\Sigma p_0 q_t$. To illustrate the advantage of this 'adding-up' property, consider consumers' expenditure. At current prices, total consumers' expenditure is the sum of expenditures on food, housing, fuel and light, and so on. Exactly the same is true of the Laspeyres quantity measure: total consumers' expenditure at constant prices is the sum of expenditures at constant prices on food, housing, fuel and light, and so on.

The second property is that, in a run of Laspeyres quantity index numbers, any one year can be compared with any other year, with a meaningful interpretation. The index of year t divided by the index of years s gives the comparison from s to t:

$$\text{Year } t \text{ on year } s \text{ as } 100 = \frac{Q_{0t}(p_0)}{Q_{0s}(p_0)} 100 = \frac{\Sigma p_0 q_t}{\Sigma p_0 q_s} 100$$

The interpretation: the changing cost at constant (year 0) prices from year s to year t.

It may be objected that the prices of year 0 have nothing to do with the years s and t compared. This is a valid objection, particularly when year 0 is in the remote past. If years 0, s and t are closer together, the ratio above is a good approximation to the quantity change from year s to year t. It gets progressively worse as time goes on from the past year 0. For example, the change in real consumers' expenditure from 1977 to 1978 is well represented by values at constant (1975) prices, less well by values at

1970 prices and quite impossible at (say) 1938 prices. But all that this implies is that an index on a fixed base – and any such index – is a short-run construction, good in the short period but not in the longer run. The long-run answer, as pursued in 7·5 below, is to string together in some appropriate way a whole series of different index numbers, first on one base, then on another base, and so on.

The computation of the Laspeyres quantity index in practice can be direct from the definition (1.1) if the cross-valuation $\Sigma p_0 q_t$ at constant prices is possible and convenient. The alternative is to use the equivalent form (1.2) as derived:

$$\frac{\Sigma p_0 q_t}{\Sigma p_0 q_0} = \frac{\Sigma p_0 q_0 \dfrac{q_t}{q_0}}{\Sigma p_0 q_0} = \frac{\Sigma w_0 \dfrac{q_t}{q_0}}{\Sigma w_0} \qquad (w_0 = p_0 q_0)$$

Here w_0 are the base values used as *weights* applied to quantity *relatives* q_t/q_0, obtained by taking current quantities as the ratio of base quantities item by item. This weighted average form is often more convenient in practice. This is clearly so when the actual quantities cannot be expressed for some items and when some approximation to the quantity relative is used. A simple example of computation is given in 6.5 below.

The *Laspeyres price index* follows by just interchanging ps and qs. It is defined by (2.1) of Table 6.1 as the changing cost of a fixed (year 0) 'basket' of items. It can be computed as a ratio of constant-quantity aggregates or as the weighted-average from (2.2) with the same weights w_0 as for the Laspeyres quantity index.

6.3 Paasche Form

In a purely formal way, Paasche or current-weighted forms are defined and computed as for Laspeyres forms: just take the constant prices or quantities from the current year t instead of the base year 0. The *Paasche quantity index* $Q_{0t}(p_t)$ is defined by (3.1) of Table 6.1 as the ratio of values at the same (year t) prices; the *Paasche price index* $p_{0t}(q_t)$ is defined by (4.1) in terms of the changing cost of the fixed (year t) 'basket' of items. If a cross-valued aggregate (e.g. $\Sigma p_0 q_t$) is taken by itself, the 'adding-up' property still holds as for the current-price aggregate (e.g. $\Sigma p_t q_t$). Unfortunately this is now of less help: the cross-valuations appear in the denominator instead of the numerator.

Difficulties emerge in handling a run of Paasche index numbers and, in particular, in the comparison of two years s and t independently of the base year 0. Take the quantity index $Q_{0t}(p_t)$. Both the numerator and the denominator vary with t and it is not possible, as it was with the Laspeyres form, to run one of them alone as the real measure. It follows that each Paasche index is a one-off comparison with the base year. Two index numbers in the run, say $Q_{0s}(p_s)$ and $Q_{0t}(p_t)$, make quite different comparison with year 0, one using constant prices of year s and the other those of year t. It is quite possible for the prices to change so that, though all quantities increase from s to t, yet the Paasche index decreases. Hence, in a Paasche index run, each index is to be used only in a comparison with the base year.

These considerations seem to rule out the Paasche form in practice. There is, however, one result of great practical use which serves to put Paasche index numbers back on the map. The result is the one which solves the problem posed at the outset, that of the split of the value change V_{0t} into quantity and price components:

$$V_{0t} = Q_{0t}(p_0) \times P_{0t}(q_t) = Q_{0t}(p_t) \times P_{0t}(q_0) \qquad \text{(A)}$$

The result follows from the definitions of Table 6.1.

There are two matching pairs of price/quantity index numbers. One of each pair is of Laspeyres form, the other a Paasche index. Specifically, the Laspeyres quantity index and the Paasche price index multiply out to the value change; between them they account precisely for the value movement. Similarly, the matching pair of the Laspeyres price and Paasche quantity index numbers provides a split of the value change.

Suppose the Laspeyres quantity measure is taken as the basic concept and computed either as $\Sigma p_0 q_t$ or as the index $Q_{0t}(p_0)$. The results are similar if the Laspeyres price index is selected as the starting point. Thus from the result (A) above:

$$\left. \begin{array}{l} V_{0t} = Q_{0t}(p_0) \times P_{0t}(q_t) \\ \text{or:} \quad \Sigma p_t q_t = \Sigma p_0 q_t \times P_{0t}(q_t) \end{array} \right\} \qquad \text{(B)}$$

The only difference between the two is that the base value $\Sigma p_0 q_0$ is removed from the denominators of V_{0t} and $Q_{0t}(p_0)$ in the second version. (B) shows that the value at current prices, or the value change, is got by multiplying the selected quantity measure by the Paasche price index. Put another way:

The match of $Q_{0t}(p_0) = \dfrac{\Sigma p_0 q_t}{\Sigma p_0 q_0}$ is $P_{0t}(q_t) = \dfrac{\Sigma p_t q_t}{\Sigma p_0 q_t} = \dfrac{V_{0t}}{Q_{0t}(p_0)}$ (C)

Because of these results, the Paasche price index is described as of *implied form*, and is so shown in Table 6.1. It is the price index implied by the Laspeyres quantity measure in the sense that the two match in accounting for the value change. Once the Laspeyres quantity index is computed, the implied (Paasche) price index follows without further calculation than simple division into the value change.

There is one particular use of the implied index: as a *deflator* to reduce a value or value change to real terms. Suppose the Laspeyres quantity measure is required either as $\Sigma p_0 q_t$ or as $Q_{0t}(p_0)$. It may be easier to take values at current prices, either $\Sigma p_t q_t$ or V_{0t}, and to deflate by division by a price index. By (B), the price index used should be the Paasche form.

A final question: what is the difference between the Laspeyres and Paasche forms? From (A) it follows that the ratio of the Paasche to Laspeyres form is the same for the price as for the quantity index. This common ratio, by a well-known result, is found to depend on a correlation between price and quantity relatives. In broad terms, the Laspeyres index is the greater of the two on a market dominated by buyers and it is the smaller on a market where supply dominates. The actual difference, as opposed to the direction, may be great or small; but a large difference is only likely when there are great shifts in the distribution of the value aggregate over its components, between years 0 and t, as when a war or an event such as the rise in oil prices at the end of 1973 intervenes.

6.4 Index Numbers in the National Accounts

Once the national accounts have been prepared at current prices, the next objective must be to eliminate the effect of price movements and to get the real or quantitative changes, in various totals and components from one year to another, identified and measured. It is also useful to have the related estimates of price changes. But this is a subsidiary matter; there are many sources of information on prices – if not of quantities – and they are generally both more frequent and more timely than the national accounts statistics.

The basic result (A) of 6.3 above gives two pairs of matching quantity/price index numbers. The task of computing one of these pairs for such data as those of the national accounts is a massive one. To compute both pairs – and so to see exactly how they differ – may be a prohibitively difficult task. So a choice may need to be made between the two pairs, at least for a routine year-by-year exercise.

For the national accounts, with their emphasis on the real movements which lie behind the money figures, the choice must be made and there is no doubt about it. The main indicator to be computed must be the Laspeyres quantity measure, to be shown usually as constant-price valuations rather than in index form. This provides an immediate and simple measure of real changes between any two years not too far apart. For example, the rise in real consumers' expenditure between 1977 and 1978 is seen from a run of expenditures at constant (1975) prices.

Consequently, the prime need is to have two runs over the years for any national income total or component:

(1) $\Sigma p_t q_t$ = value at current prices in each year t
(2) $\Sigma p_0 q_t$ = value at constant (year 0) prices in each year t

Here (1) is already available once the national accounts are put together for year t. The cross-valuations of (2) are those to be computed. To get quantity index numbers in explicit Laspeyres form: divide through the run (2) by the base value $\Sigma p_0 q_0$.

The useful but subsidiary task of estimating the related price changes is easily accomplished. The price index to obtain is the implied index of Paasche form, the index which combines with the quantity run (2) to account for value changes. No additional computations are needed. All that has to be done is to use formula (C) of 6.3 above; this is just a matter of dividing the entry in run (1) for year t by the corresponding entry in run (2).

The implied price index numbers inherit the problems of the one-off property of the Paasche form (6.3 above). If 1975 is the base year, for example, an implied price index for consumers' expenditure gives a valid comparison of prices in 1977 or in 1978 with 1975, but not between 1977 and 1978. Given the decision to compute only one pair of index numbers, one of them is of Laspeyres form with ready comparisons between any years and the other has the limitations of the Paasche form. It is important to be able to make real comparisons, e.g. between real consumers' expenditure in any two years. It needs to be accepted, as a consequence, that the corresponding price comparisons are less good.

The decision to compute only one pair of quantity/price index numbers may be dictated by practical considerations. There remains a valid criticism of the decision. The Laspeyres quantity index which is computed is different from the Paasche quantity index which is not. The difference may be either way, e.g. the computed (Laspeyres) index is likely to be the higher for consumers' expenditure since demand usually dominates, but lower for agricultural output where supply can dominate. It is not likely to be large – but can be quite substantial for years around 1973 when oil prices rose sharply. Moreover, the implied price index of Paasche form differs in the same way, but opposite direction, from the unpublished Laspeyres price index. For example, of the pair of index numbers calculated for consumers' expenditure, that for real consumers' expenditure is likely to be *higher* than its mate in the other pair, while that for consumers' price is likely to be *lower* than its opposite number. If real consumers' expenditure is overstated by the choice of the Laspeyres quantity index, it follows that the implied (Paasche) price index is an understatement of price rises.

6.5 An Example

Statistics of UK exports of merchandise provide detailed figures for the illustration of the calculation of matching pairs of quantity/price index numbers. To bring the example within the scope of calculations by hand, one small sub-group of exports is taken here: dairy produce and eggs. The published data for 1976 and 1977 are in Table 6.2, together with the calculations needed for estimating the Laspeyres quantity index and the implied price index in 1977 with 1976 as 100.

Take 1976 as year 0 and 1977 as year t. The cross-valuation needed is $\Sigma p_0 q_t$, obtained by first writing p_0 in column (3) and then by multiplying by the given q_t of column (4). The prices here are unit values, not price quotations (see 6.7 below). This can be set out as in Table 6.3. Each of the index numbers is arrived at by division and multiplication by 100:

Quantity $\dfrac{88,731}{114,995} 100 = 77 \cdot 2$ Price $\dfrac{97,958}{88,731} 100 = 110 \cdot 4$

Value $\dfrac{97,958}{114,995} 100 = 85 \cdot 2$

The value split, formula (B) of 6.3 above, with the 100 factor omitted, is as follows:

$$V_{0t} = Q_{0t}(p_0) \times P_{0t}(q_t): \quad 0 \cdot 852 = 0 \cdot 772 \times 1 \cdot 104$$

TABLE 6.2 UK exports of dairy produce and eggs: calculation of $\Sigma p_0 q_t$

Commodity	1976 Quantity 000 tonnes q_0 (1)	1976 Value £000 $p_0 q_0$ (2)	Unit value (2)/(1) £ per tonne p_0 (3)	1977 Quantity 000 tonnes q_t (4)	1977 Value £000 $p_t q_t$ (5)	Cross-valuation £000 $p_0 q_t$ (3) × (4)
Milk and cream:						
evaporated	30.8	8608	279	48.7	14510	13587
dried	143.9	67945	472	77.8	40735	36722
fresh	54.4	2559	47.0	29.2	2323	1372
Butter	16.0	18071	1129	14.5	17329	16370
Cheese	10.7	9158	856	10.8	11445	9245
Eggs	11.8	8654	733	15.6	11616	11435
Total		114995			97958	88731

SOURCE
Overseas Trade Statistics, annual issues for 1976 and 1977.

TABLE 6.3 UK exports of dairy produce and eggs

	1976	1977
(1) Value at current prices (£000)	114995	97958
(2) Value at constant (1976) prices (£000)	114995	88731
Laspeyres quantity index. From (2) (1976 = 100)	100	77·2
Implied (Paasche) price index. From (1)/(2)		
(1976 = 100)	100	110·4
Value change. From (1) (1976 = 100)	100	85·2

On this pair of index numbers, a fall of 32·8 per cent in exports, partly offset by a price rise of 10·4 per cent, gave a fall of 14·8 per cent in value of exports from 1976 to 1977.

This may seem to be a trivial example since the UK can scarcely be described as an exporter of dairy produce. But there are considerable exports of dried milk and some trade between Northern Ireland and the Irish Republic. In any case, the calculation is necessary as part of the computation of index numbers of wider scope, for exports of food and then of all items. It is also a good illustration of methods since these particular exports are very variable in price and quantity from one year to another.

The alternative and equivalent calculation of the quantity index is set out in Table 6.4. The weights are written for convenience – and as usual

TABLE 6.4 UK exports of dairy produce and eggs: calculation of Laspeyres quantity index

Commodity	Weights w_0 (1)	Quantity relative q_t/q_0 (2)	Product (1) × (2)
Milk and cream:			
evaporated	75	158·1	11858
dried	591	54·1	31973
fresh	22	53·7	1181
Butter	157	90·6	14224
Cheese	80	100·9	8072
Eggs	75	132·2	9915
Total	1000		77223

SOURCE

Column (1): Table 6.2, column (2), expressed per 1000.
Column (2): Table 6.2, column (1) and (4), q_t expressed as % of q_0.

in practice – per 1000 of the value (£114,995) of 1976 exports, and rounded to the nearest digit. This is in order since w_0 appears both in the numerator and in the denominator of the weighted average; only proportionate values are needed. So:

$$\text{Laspeyres quantity index } \frac{\text{Total (1)} \times (2)}{\text{Total (1)}} = \frac{77,223}{1000} = 77 \cdot 2$$

and the implied price index follows as before to make up the value change.

The other pair of matching index numbers comes from the cross-valuation $\Sigma p_t q_0$, as calculated in Table 6.5. This value is the cost of the fixed (1976) 'basket' of exports at the prices of 1977. Taken with the current values shown in Table 6.2, it gives:

TABLE 6.5 UK exports of dairy produce and eggs: calculation of $\Sigma p_t q_0$

Commodity	1976 Quantity 000 tonnes q_0 (1)	1977 Unit value £ per tonne p_t (2)	Product (1) × (2)
Milk and Cream:			
evaporated	30·8	298	9178
dried	143·9	524	75404
fresh	54·4	79·6	4330
Butter	16·0	1195	19120
Cheese	10·7	1060	11342
Eggs	11·8	745	8791
Total			128165

SOURCE
Table 6.2, columns (1), (4) and (5).

$$\text{Laspeyres price index } \quad \frac{\Sigma p_t q_0}{\Sigma p_0 q_0} 100 = \frac{128,165}{114,995} 100 = 111 \cdot 5$$

$$\text{Implied (Paasche) quantity index } \frac{\Sigma p_t q_t}{\Sigma p_t q_0} 100 = \frac{97,958}{128,165} 100 = 76 \cdot 4$$

Both are for 1977 with 1976 as 100. Again they split the value change; the equation is now: $0 \cdot 852 = 0 \cdot 764 \times 1 \cdot 115$. Between the two pairs, the

Laspeyres quantity index exceeds the Paasche form by a modest and quite acceptable amount, and similarly for the two price index numbers. From the alternative pairs, and after rounding off, it is possible to say that the fall of 15 per cent in the value of exports from 1976 to 1977 is the result of a decline of about 23 per cent by volume and a rise of some 11 per cent in prices.

6.6 Estimation when Quantity Data Lacking

A value aggregate often includes items not sufficiently homogeneous for the specification of quantities. Some kind of approximation is then needed in estimating a quantity index number. Take the index as a weighted average of quantity relatives, q_t/q_0, some of which are unknown and for which substitutes need to be found. A common device is to substitute a value change deflated by a specially constructed index of prices for the item in question. If the required quantity index is of Laspeyres form, the deflator should be a Paasche price index (6.3 above). This is not always possible in practice and it is sometimes necessary to make do with a deflator of Laspeyres form.

As an illustration, suppose that eggs are given by value only in the example of 6.5 above. (This is not far-fetched since the item 'eggs' may be a souffle of shell eggs, egg yolks, dried eggs and other forms.) In the calculation of Table 6.4, the quantity relative for eggs is missing and something must be found to put in its place. The usual substitute is the value of exports (Table 6.2) deflated by an index of egg prices. An index is to hand: the Ministry of Agriculture's index of the average prices paid to producers of shell eggs at packing stations (see Table 6.6).

TABLE 6.6   UK exports of eggs: a substitute quantity relative

	1976	1977
Exports of eggs, value at current prices (£000)	8654	11616
Index of egg prices (1976 = 100)	100	114·5
Deflated value of exports, at 1976 prices (£000)	8654	10147*
Substitute quantity relative (1976 = 100)	100	117·2

NOTE
* Obtained by division of 11616 by the index 1·145 (without the 100).

On substituting 117·2 for the quantity relative for eggs in Table 6·4 and on recalculating the sum of products, the estimated Laspeyres quantity index is 76·1. This approximate figure is considerably different from the index actually obtained (77.2) from Table 6.4. It indicates the need for a better price deflator, e.g. an index of Paasche form using prices of dried eggs and other egg products as well as shell eggs.

There is an alternative method of substituting for missing quantity data which is sometimes used in practice. It is to divide a value aggregate into fairly small categories and to assume that an item without quantity data has a *price* movement identical with that found for the rest of the category in which the item falls. The assumption here is the reasonable one that, for items in a single category, price movements are more likely to be in line than quantity movements.

The application of this method turns out to be quite simple. Write values and index numbers for all items in the category, except the one with quantities lacking, by symbols with a prime; the unknown complete values and index numbers for the category appear without the prime. Let the matching pair of index numbers be the Laspeyres quantity index Q_{0t} and the Paasche price index P_{0t}, accounting for the value change. Then, with and without the item with quantity data lacking:

$$V_{0t} = Q_{0t} \times P_{0t} \quad \text{and} \quad V'_{0t} = Q'_{0t} \times P'_{0t}$$

giving

$$\frac{Q_{0t}}{Q'_{0t}} = \frac{V_{0t}}{V'_{0t}} \times \frac{P'_{0t}}{P_{0t}} = \frac{V_{0t}}{V'_{0t}}$$

since the price movement of the missing item is assumed to be P'_{0t}, so ensuring that the complete P_{0t} is also P'_{0t}. Hence, from the computation of Q'_{0t} and P'_{0t} for the category (minus the item with quantity lacking), the complete values follow:

$$Q_{0t} = \frac{V_{0t}}{V'_{0t}} \times Q'_{0t} \quad \text{and} \quad P_{0t} = P'_{0t}$$

In the example of 6.5, V_{0t} for 1977 is 85·2 per cent of 1976. Assume that eggs are given by value only and that their price moves in the same way as the other items in the category (dairy produce and eggs). On omitting eggs from the calculations of Table 6.2, the following totals are obtained:

$$\Sigma' p_0 q_0 = 106{,}341 \qquad \Sigma' p_t q_t = 86{,}342 \qquad \Sigma' p_0 q_t = 77{,}296$$

giving

$$V_{0t}' = \frac{86,342}{106,341}100 = 81\cdot2 \quad \text{Laspeyres } Q_{0t}' = \frac{77,296}{106,341}100 = 72\cdot7$$

$$\text{Paasche } P_{0t}' = \frac{86,342}{77,296}100 = 111\cdot7$$

Hence the estimates for all items are:

$$\text{Laspeyres } Q_{0t} = \frac{V_{0t}}{V_{0t}'}Q_{0t}' = \frac{85\cdot2}{81\cdot2}72\cdot7 = 76\cdot3$$

and

$$\text{Paasche } P_{0t} = P_{0t}' = 111\cdot7$$

These are still a good way off the correct values but a little closer than on the first method.

6.7 Price Quotations or Unit Values?

In the split of a value into quantity and price components by means of index numbers, the price index should relate to 'pure' price quotations, leaving the quantity index to measure changes *both* in the number of units (e.g. numbers or tonnes) *and* in the quality of the items. An increase in real consumers' expenditure, for example, may well represent *both* more *and* better TV sets.

National accounts statistics often use, as in the example of 6.5, 'prices' which are not price quotations but unit values derived by dividing value by quantity in a more or less homogeneous item. Changes in unit values can reflect changes in both price quotations and the quality and make-up of the item, e.g. a shift from cheaper to dearer goods. The latter changes will go through to the 'price' index and not, as they should, to the quantity index. It is not only that the 'price' index shows too much; the quantity index fails to include all that should be in it. When commodities are improving in quality, the risk is that the 'price' index runs high and the quantity index low.

It all depends on how close unit values are as indicators of price quotations for types and qualities strictly unchanged over time. As a fairly extreme case, take the example of Table 6.2 and run all items together in tonnes. The results are as shown in Table 6.7. The unit value

TABLE 6.7 UK exports of dairy produce and eggs: calculation of overall unit values

	1976	1977	1977 as % of 1976
Total quantity (000 tonnes)	267·6	196·6	73·5
Total value (£000)	114995	97958	85·2
Unit value (£ per tonne)	429·7	498·3	116·0

SOURCE
Table 6.2.

index in 1977, 116·0 per cent of 1976, must include a good deal of the effect of shifting composition of this (very non-homogeneous) category. It is, in fact, a good deal higher than the index got from Table 6.2 (110·4 per cent of 1976) on the basis of unit values of more homogeneous sub-groups. The corresponding quantity index is low, 73·5 as compared with 77·2 per cent of 1976.

Little can be said in general on what should be done. In some cases, an index of unit values is acceptable because items are homogeneous or because different brands or qualities move together. In other cases, a unit-values index needs to be accepted because of the lack of any alternative even when quality shifts are known to occur. There are, however, other cases where something can be done, e.g. by basing a unit-values index on fine and homogeneous sub-divisions of items. The example of Table 6.2 goes some way in this direction and could be taken further. A method often used is to give up quantities and unit values altogether; instead carefully weighted index numbers of available price quotations for small categories are designed, if possible of Paasche form. The recorded value in each category is deflated by its price index to give substitute quantities for use in a Laspeyres weighted-average computation (as in Table 6.3). There are many cases where deflated values are preferable to physical quantities.

7 Real GDP: Three Measures

7.1 Real GDP(E): Components

There are three measures of GDP in real terms to match the three measures at current prices (2.5 above). They are respectively from the side of expenditure, income and output and denoted as GDP(E), GDP(I) and GDP(O). All measures are index numbers; those used for illustration here are based on 1975 and run from 1973 to 1978.

The measure from the expenditure side is considered first. GDP(E) and its components at current prices are described and illustrated in 3.3 above. Then the decision is taken (6.4 above) to take real GDP(E) as an index of Laspeyres form, matched with a price index of implied (Paasche) form. What is needed to implement this decision, for each component of GDP(E) in year t, is the calculation of the cross-valuation $\Sigma p_0 q_t$ at the constant prices of a selected base year 0 to set alongside the valuation $\Sigma p_t q_t$ at current prices.

Table 7.1 shows the main components of GDP(E), in the top part at current prices as in 3.3 above and in the bottom part at constant (1975) prices on revaluing current quantities at the prices of 1975. All values are at market prices before reduction to factor cost by deduction of net indirect taxes.

The components of real GDP(E) are the values at constant (1975) prices, as given in Table 7.1 in £ million. It is a simple matter to convert them to Laspeyres index numbers based on 1975: just divide through by the 1975 value. So, real consumers' expenditure, in £ million at 1975 prices, is to be read off the first line of the lower part of the table. The percentage change from one year to another is easily derived: there is (e.g.) a fall of 0·6 per cent in real consumption from 1975 to 1977, given by comparing 63,704 with 63,313 (£million at 1975 prices). Expressed as a Laspeyres quantity index:

$$\text{Real consumption 1977 (1975} = 100): \frac{\Sigma p_0 q_t}{\Sigma p_0 q_0} 100 = \frac{63,313}{63,704} 100 = 99 \cdot 4$$

which again shows the decline of 0·6 per cent.

TABLE 7.1 Components of GDP(E) (in £ millions at market prices)

	1973	1974	1975	1976	1977	1978
At current prices:						
Consumers' expenditure	45472	52088	63704	73765	84132	96086
Government final consumption	13327	16558	23050	26683	29167	32693
Gross domestic capital formation[1]	15711	18181	19068	24244	27582	30746
Exports of goods and services[2]	17301	23106	27145	35435	43735	47636
less imports of goods and services[2]	−18978	−27395	−29018	−36779	−42488	−45522
less net indirect taxes	−8679	−8465	−10447	−13080	−16917	−19640
At 1975 prices:						
Consumers' expenditure	65911	64418	63704	63852	63313	66728
Government final consumption	21426	21732	23050	23477	23268	23623
Gross domestic capital formation[1]	24154	22291	19068	21059	21404	21614
Exports of goods and services[2]	26109	27823	27145	29611	31679	32343
less imports of goods and services[2]	−31052	−31318	−29018	−30184	−30405	−31626
less adjustment to factor cost[3]	−10914	−10633	−10447	−10857	−10842	−11857

Including increase in stocks (in £ millions)	*1973*	*1974*	*1975*	*1976*	*1977*	*1978*
at current prices	1504	1255	−1477	642	1669	1528
at 1975 prices	3043	1655	−1477	436	1217	1129

NOTES
[1] Including increase in stocks (in £ millions)
[2] Valued as in balance of payments, i.e. exports include but imports exclude net indirect taxes.
[3] The difference between taxes on expenditure and subsidies each revalued at 1975 rates of tax and subsidy.
SOURCE
1979 *Blue Book*, Tables 1.1 and 2.1.

The general movement in real GDP(E) components is clear from the lower part of Table 7.1: a fall from 1973 to the depression year 1975 and a recovery to 1978. But government final consumption increased throughout, except for a small fall in 1977 which also showed up in consumers' expenditure. Exports also increased over the whole period apart from a bad year in 1975.

The valuations of Table 7.1 have an adding-up property, equally at constant as at current prices. For example, to get total domestic expenditure for entry in Table 7.2 below: add the first three components of GDP(E). This can be done at current prices (top of Table 7.1) and at 1975 prices (bottom of the table). Further, any of the components can be split into finer and finer groups and sub-groups either at constant or at current prices. This is done in great detail in the tables of the *Blue Book*. For example Table 4.9 shows consumers' expenditure at current prices in main groups such as food and clothing and in sub-groups such as fish and footwear; Table 4.10 then gives the same expenditures in real terms at 1975 prices.

A major technical question remains: in practice, how is the cross-valuation $\Sigma p_0 q_t$ for the various components to be arrived at year by year? The obvious method is to use disaggregated price/quantity data as in the example of Table 6.2 above. This simple method often fails either because quantity data are lacking (6.6 above) or because the prices are unit values affected by quality changes (6.7 above). There are several ways out of these difficulties and two are used extensively.

One device is to start from the base year expenditure $p_0 q_0$ on an item and to adjust for quantity changes to year t by the formula $p_0 q_t = p_0 q_0 \left(\dfrac{q_t}{q_0} \right)$. If the quantities q_0 and q_t cannot be given in appropriate units directly, an approximation may be possible by finding some indicator of the change q_t/q_0. For example, expenditure on newspapers uses an index of newspaper circulation.

The second device, even more commonly employed, is to start from the current expenditure $p_t q_t$ on an item and to adjust for price changes from the base year by the formula $p_0 q_t = p_t q_t \left/ \dfrac{p_t}{p_0} \right.$. This is the method of deflation of current values by an indicator of price changes p_t/p_0. The deflator usually takes the form of a specially constructed price index which should be (6.3 above) of Paasche form. This is increasingly so in practice but it is still true that many deflators are of Laspeyres type. This may serve well enough since Laspeyres and Paasche forms are seldom far apart (6.3 above) and the difference is likely to be quite small for a single item which is fairly homogeneous.

All this adds up to a practical problem of great complexity. The methods adopted by the Central Statistical Office are described in *Sources and Methods* and in such subsequent articles as 'An Assessment of the Sensitivity of the National Accounts Constant Price Estimates', *Economic Trends*, No. 244, February 1974. See also 7.6 below for the base change from 1970 to 1975.

As a broad assessment it can be said that most groups of consumers' expenditure are quite accurately valued at constant prices, whereas corresponding values for government final consumption and gross domestic capital formation are often rougher approximations. Government final consumption (2.3 above) is not purchases of government services by consumers but purchases by central and local government of goods and services including the pay of government employees. In the valuation (e.g.) of NHS expenditures at constant prices, use is made of such indicators as numbers of prescriptions. Here and elsewhere, some of the cross-valuation depends on employment series, either numbers employed or wages/salaries bills deflated by rates of pay, and so needs to assume no change in productivity (see *Sources and Methods*, pp. 356–9). The reduction of values of exports and imports to constant prices raises particular problems. There is here a mix of very detailed calculations for goods and the much rougher estimates which have to be accepted for services (see 8.4 below).

7.2 Real GDP(E): Totals

Consumers' expenditure, government final consumption and gross domestic capital formation together make up total domestic expenditure. The steps from this total to GDP at factor cost are shown in Table 3.4 above at current prices. The same process is followed at constant prices and the results are given in Table 7.2. Any one of these series at 1975 prices can be displayed, by division through by the 1975 value, as a run of Laspeyres quantity index numbers. They are shown in Table 7.3.

There are substantial differences between the variations over time of total domestic expenditure, total final expenditure and GDP at constant market prices. They arise because of different movements in the volume of exports and of imports of goods and services. For example, exports recovered more than imports after 1975 and real exports had gone well ahead of real imports in 1977/78. As a result total domestic expenditure (excluding exports, including imports) increased by only 6 per cent in real

TABLE 7.2 GDP(E): expenditure totals (in £ millions)

	1973	1974	1975	1976	1977	1978
At current prices:						
Total domestic expenditure*	74510	86827	105822	124692	140881	159525
Total final expenditure*	91811	109933	132967	160127	184616	207161
GDP at market prices	72833	82538	103949	123348	142128	161639
GDP at factor cost	64154	74073	93502	110268	125211	141999
At 1975 prices:						
Total domestic expenditure*	111491	108441	105822	108388	107985	111965
Total final expenditure*	137600	136264	132967	137999	139664	144308
GDP at market prices	106548	104946	103949	107815	109259	112682
GDP at factor cost	95634	94313	93502	96958	98417	100825

NOTE
* At market prices.
SOURCE
Table 7.1, above.

TABLE 7.3 GDP(E): quantity and implied price index numbers (1975 = 100)

Index number of:	1973	1974	1975	1976	1977	1978
Quantity:						
Total domestic expenditure*	105·4	102·5	100	102·4	102·0	105·8
Total final expenditure*	103·5	102·5	100	103·8	105·0	108·5
GDP at market prices	102·5	101·0	100	103·7	105·1	108·4
GDP at factor cost	102·3	100·9	100	103·7	105·3	107·8
Price:						
GDP deflator	67·1	78·5	100	113·7	127·2	140·8

NOTE
* At market prices.
SOURCE
Table 7.2 above. Quantity index numbers of Laspeyres form; GDP deflator Paasche index implied by real GDP at factor cost.

terms in 1975–8 whereas GDP at constant market prices (including exports, excluding imports) rose by more than 8 per cent.

The year-to-year changes in real GDP are much the same whether measured at market prices or at factor cost and it is important to see why this is so. At current prices GDP at market prices exceeds GDP at factor cost by net indirect taxes. The difference is variable over time, being sensitive to changes in the rates of indirect taxes and subsidies. At constant prices, however, the effect of changing rates of taxes and subsidies is eliminated. The adjustment to factor cost varies little from one year to another (Table 7.1) and real GDP at market prices and at factor cost move almost in parallel. Put another way, real GDP at market prices is measured by $\Sigma p_0 q_t$ and at factor cost by $\Sigma p_0' q_t$. Here p_0 is the market price and p_0' the factor cost in the base year of an item whose quantity q_t varies over time. The q_ts are exactly the same in the two measures; only the basic prices used for combining them are different. In real GDP at market prices, more weight is given to items like petrol with high taxes (and high p_0); in real GDP at factor cost, the heavy weights go to subsidised items such as milk. The two measures of real GDP can only differ significantly if the quantities purchased of highly taxed and highly subsidised items diverge over time. This rarely happens. It is not surprising that the two index numbers of real GDP in Table 7.3 do not differ by more than 0·6 percentage points.

To each quantity measure of Laspeyres form there is a matching price index of implied (Paasche) form, to be calculated from formula (4.1) of Table 6.1 above: $\Sigma p_t q_t / p_0 q_t$. Tables 7.1 and 7.2 are designed to provide the price index numbers as well as the quantity measures. (The bottom parts of the tables are enough for the quantity measures.) The implied price index comes from dividing an entry in the top part of a table ($\Sigma p_t q_t$) by the corresponding entry in the bottom part ($\Sigma p_0 q_t$).

The derivation and use of the price index numbers are left to 8.1 below. Meanwhile the calculation is illustrated by arriving at one particular price index needed in this chapter: the index implied by real GDP at factor cost. It is shown in Table 7.3 with the title *GDP deflator*. An alternative title is the index of *home costs per unit of output*. It is got by dividing GDP at current factor cost by the corresponding figure at 1975 factor cost. For example:

$$\text{GDP deflator 1976 (1975 = 100):} \frac{\Sigma p_t q_t}{\Sigma p_0 q_t} 100 = \frac{110{,}268}{96{,}958} 100 = 113 \cdot 7$$

This index is much used (e.g.) as one possible measure of inflation (8.3 below).

7.3 Real GDP(O): Laspeyres Index

GDP(O) at current factor cost is the sum of values added industry by industry as shown in Table 3·8 above. An industry's value added is the difference between gross output and the input of goods and services from other industries or from abroad; it equals the sum of factor incomes (wages, salaries, rents and profits) generated in the industry. The object now is to get GDP(O) in real terms. Since this is an output measure – and not from the income side – the exercise is to reduce value added, as the excess of gross output over input, from current to constant factor cost. The question arises: what is meant by value added at constant factor cost?

The answer coming nearest to the economists' concept leads to the method of *double deflation*. For an industry:

Value added at constant factor cost = gross output at constant
$$\text{output prices } \textit{less} \text{ input} \quad \text{(A)}$$
at constant input prices

The method is used by several Continental countries, at least for much of GDP(O), but in this country only for agriculture. The practical difficulty arises from the fact that the two terms of (A) are large aggregates subject to errors of estimation. When the difference is taken, the errors remain in absolute terms and they are large relative to the (often quite small) difference. Real value added by double deflation may be subject to unacceptably large errors. There may well be industries with substantial value added at current factor cost but turned into an estimate of real value added which is negative.

An alternative and more practical calculation starts by giving up any attempt to get real GDP(O) as a constant-price valuation in £million, like GDP(E), and by returning to the base-weighted (Laspeyres) index:

$$\text{Real GDP(0):} \quad \frac{1}{\Sigma w_0} \Sigma w_0 \frac{q_t}{q_0} \text{ in year } t \text{ (base year 0)} \quad \text{(B)}$$

This is formula (1.2) of Table 6.1 above but now Σ is summation over industries, w_0 is the value added by an industry in the base year and q_t/q_0 is an indicator of the change in value added at constant factor cost. On the double deflation method q_t is simply (A) above and q_0 is w_0. On the approximate method used for industries other than agriculture, the indicator q_t/q_0 is taken usually as the change in gross output by quantity (ignoring input) or sometimes as the change in real input (ignoring output). Such an indicator correctly represents changes in an industry's value added in real terms only if the ratio of input to gross output remains constant. The ratio can, however, vary considerably over time. In some industries it may decrease (e.g.) because of more economical use of materials; in other industries it may increase (e.g.) because more of the work gets contracted out. Gross output as an indicator can understate the increase in real value added (in the first case), or there can be an overstatement (as in the second case).

In the use of (B) for real GDP(O) it must be expected that real output is understated in some sectors of the economy and overstated in others. On balance the total index and its main components may not be far out. But this depends heavily on specifying a fine categorisation by industry, with good estimates of value-added weights w_0, and then on getting the best indicator q_t/q_0 from data available regularly over time. The construction of the index is described in Central Statistical Office, *The Measurement of Changes in Production: Studies in Official Statistics*, no. 25 (London: HMSO, 1976). This relates to the index based on 1970; that with 1975 as base is similar (see 7.6 below). Table 7.4 shows

TABLE 7.4 GDP(O): index numbers at 1975 factor cost (1975 = 100)

Industry[1]	Weight[2]	1973	1974	1975	1976	1977	1978
Agriculture, etc.	28	109	110	100	93	111	116
Industrial production	407	110·1	105·7	100	102·5	106·5	110·2
Transport, etc.	88	100	101	100	99	102	106
Distributive trades	101	107	103	100	101	99	104
Banking, finance, etc.	73	97	99	100	102	103	106
Ownership of dwellings	61	96	98	100	102	104	106
Professional and scientific	129	91	95	100	104	105	107
Miscellaneous services	73	105	101	100	105	106	112
Public administration and defence	80	97	97	100	104	103	102
Adjustment for financial services	−40	95	102	100	101	102	107
Real GDP(O)	1000	103·8	101·9	100	102·2	104·8	107·8

NOTES
[1] Classification as in Table 3.8 above except that government and other services are here split into professional and scientific, miscellaneous services, and public administration and defence.
[2] Value added by industry in 1975 expressed per 1000 of total.
SOURCE
1979 *Blue Book*, Table 2.2.

the main components of the 1975-based index for the years 1973–8.

There is little difficulty about the industrial classification and the weights as base values added. These come from the data summarised in Table 3.8 above, with some minor modifications indicated in the 1979 *Blue Book*, p. 112. Notice that the last item in the weights is a negative one to represent adjustment for financial services (2.7 above). This is an unusual but quite proper feature of a weighted average.

There is more difficulty on choice of indicators q_t/q_0. The variety of indicators is indicated by the following summary of the 1970-based index (the 1975-based index is not very different). About 36 per cent of the total weight is represented by indicators as quantities in specified units such as tonnes of output, passenger-miles or numbers of cheques cleared. Rather more indicators, making up 44 per cent of the total weight, are deflated values; for example, the value of clothing produced, the cost of NHS prescriptions and the value of insurance premiums. The remaining indicators, apart from the double deflation for agriculture, represent inputs either of materials or of labour. Notice that the adjustment for financial services with its negative weight needs its own indicators (e.g. numbers of mortgage advances by building societies) to show the extent of duplication eliminated.

The greatest precision is attained in the industries which make up industrial production: mining, manufacturing, construction, utilities. The index numbers here are given to one decimal place whereas those for other sectors are rounded to the nearest 1 per cent.

The adding-up property of GDP(E) becomes a more complicated process for GDP(O) and Table 7.5 provides an illustration of the part played by the weights of the index. It does two things: in A it throws together the last six components of the index into a combined category of 'other services' and in B it recalculates the real GDP(O) index from the reduced set of five components. This is of particular interest since the quarterly index of real GDP(O) on publication in *Economic Trends* is shown with only the five components of Table 7.5B. The index for 'other services' has, therefore, been got by combining six components as in Table 7.5A.

The calculations are done for 1974 with 1975 as 100, so illustrating that the index can be carried backwards as well as forwards. Each calculation follows the formula for a weighted average: form the products of weights times indicators, add and divide by the sum of weights. So, the real output index (97·1) for 'other services', entered in Column(2), is 36513 divided by 376. Similarly, real GDP(O) is 101904 divided by 1000, giving101·9 at the foot of Column (2). A backwards index of this kind needs careful interpretation. Real GDP(O) falls from

TABLE 7.5 Real GDP(O): illustrative calculations

		Weight (1)	Index 1974 1975 = 100 (2)	Product (1) × (2)
A:	Banking, finance, etc.	73	99	7227
	Ownership of dwellings	61	98	5978
	Professional and scientific	129	95	12255
	Miscellaneous services	73	101	7373
	Public administration and defence	80	97	7760
	Adjustment for financial services	−40	102	−4080
	Total: other services	376	97·1	36513
B:	Agriculture, etc.	28	110	3080
	Industrial production	407	105·7	43020
	Transport, etc.	88	101	8888
	Distributive trades	101	103	10403
	Other services	376	97·1	36513
	Real GDP(O)	1000	101·9	101904

SOURCE
Table 7.4, above.

101·9 in 1974 to 100 in 1975. The separation of 'other services' shows that the output in this sector of the economy rises from 1974 to 1975, from 97·1 to 100, in contrast to the falls in each of the other sectors of Table 7.5B.

The second component in real GDP(O) of Table 7.4 is usually considered separately as the *index of industrial production*. It accounts for a little over 40 per cent of the total weight of GDP(O). It is analysed as such in considerable industrial detail in the *Blue Book*. Moreover, it is calculated and published monthly as one of the most-quoted indicators of economic activity. The monthly index numbers, and the detail by industries, differ in one important respect from the component of real GDP(O) with the same title. Many of the indicators used for industrial production are sales or deliveries rather than output, often derived from the quarterly sales enquiries of the Business Statistics Office. Since output equals sales *plus* increase in stocks, sales indicators need to be adjusted for stock changes before being used as index numbers of output. The practical difficulty is that information on stocks is both less good and less frequent that on sales. The monthly index of industrial production is, therefore, left unadjusted, as are the industrial details in the *Blue Book*. Adjustments for stock changes are made only when the index takes its place as a component of real GDP(O). The consequence is that the annual averages of the (unadjusted) monthly index differ from the (adjusted) component of real GDP(O) (see Table 7.6). It happens that in the period covered by Table 7.6 stock increases fell off more rapidly from 1973 to 1975, and recovered more quickly thereafter, than did sales.

TABLE 7.6 Industrial production (1975 = 100)

	1973	1974	1975	1976	1977	1978
Average of monthly index	109·5	105·1	100	102·0	105·8	109·7
Component of real GDP(O)	110·1	105·7	100	102·5	106·5	110·2

7.4 Three Measures of Real GDP

The two measures of real GDP so far obtained are almost entirely independent, being calculated from different source material. It remains to obtain the third measure, that from the side of income.

From 2.5 above, as aggregates at current factor cost, the income estimate GDP(I) equals the output estimates GDP(O) and each differs from the expenditure estimate to GDP(E) by the residual error:

$$\text{GDP(I)} + \text{Residual Error} = \text{GDP(E) at current factor cost} \qquad \text{(A)}$$

Real GDP(I), as the third measure of real GDP, is derived neither as another independent estimate nor from real GDP(O). Instead it is related to expenditure data and the definition is given conscisely on p. 106 of the 1979 *Blue Book*: 'The estimate obtained by deflating the income estimate of gross domestic product at current prices by the price index implied by the current and constant price estimates based on expenditure data.' In short, the GDP deflator given in Table 7.3 is used to reduce both GDP(E) and GDP(I) to real terms. From (A):

$$\frac{\text{GDP(I)}}{\text{GDP deflator}} = \frac{\text{GDP(E)}}{\text{GDP deflator}} - \frac{\text{Residual error}}{\text{GDP deflator}}$$

and so:

$$\text{Real GDP(I)} = \text{Real GDP(E)} - \frac{\text{Residual error}}{\text{GDP deflator}} \qquad \text{(B)}$$

Hence, real GDP(I), which is given only in total, is arrived at equally by direct deflation of GDP(I) at current factor cost and by subtraction of the deflated residual error from real GDP(E).

The calculations, step by step, of the three measures of real GDP are illustrated in Table 7.7 for 1976 with 1975 as 100. The estimates obtained directly from the 1979 *Blue Book* are set out in Table 7.7A, leaving seven gaps to be filled. The first two gaps in Row (2) are filled by deflating the residual error by the GDP deflator and by using (B) to give real GDP(I) in £ million at 1975 factor cost. Row (3) is then completed by expressing real GDP(I) as an index number. Row (2) is completed

TABLE 7.7 Three measures of real GDP

				Expenditure data	*less residual error*	*Income data*	*Output data*
A:	(1)	GDP at current	1975	93502	888	92614	92614
		factor cost (£ millions)	1976	110268	1321	108947	108947
	(2)	GDP at 1975 factor					
		cost (£ millions)	1976	96958	. . .	. . .	. . .
	(3)	Real GDP					
		(1975 = 100)	1976	103·7	NA	. . .	102·2
	(4)	GDP deflator					
		(1975 = 100)	1976	113·7	. . .	. . .	. . .
B:	(1)	GDP at current	1975	93502	888	92614	92614
		factor cost (£ millions)	1976	110268	1321	108947	108947
	(2)	GDP at 1975 factor					
		cost (£ millions)	1976	96958	1162	95796	94652
	(3)	Real GDP					
		(1975 = 100)	1976	103·7	NA	103·4	102·2
	(4)	GDP deflator					
		(1975 = 100)	1976	113·7	113·7	113·7	*

. . . to be derived.

NA not applicable.

* Can be calculated: $\dfrac{108{,}947}{94{,}652}100 = 115\cdot1$; but see 8.1 below.

SOURCE OF A
1979 *Blue Book*. Table 1.2 for the two Rows (1); Table 2.1 for Row (2); Tables 2.1 and 2.2 for Row (3); Table 2.5 for Row (4).

by calculating real GDP(O) in £ million at 1975 factor cost, i.e. by multiplying the real GDP(O) index of Row (3) by the 1975 value of Row (1). Finally, in Row (4), the GDP deflator of the first column is inserted in the next two, leaving the last entry (which can also be derived) for later consideration. The final result is Table 7.7B.

The three measures of real GDP in 1976 (1975 = 100) are the entries in Row (3) of Table 7.7B. The measures for the years 1973–8 are shown in Table 7.8. If a single estimate is needed, the arithmetic average of the three is taken, as given in Table 7.8. These index numbers for real GDP, and their average, are published regularly, quarterly as well as annually, in the press releases from the Central Statistical Office, in *Economic Trends* and in the *Blue Book*. As for current price estimates (3.1 above), the quarterly index numbers are adjusted for seasonal variation.

TABLE 7.8 GDP: index numbers at 1975 factor cost (1975 = 100)

	1973	1974	1975	1976	1977	1978
Based on:						
expenditure data	102·3	100·9	100	103·7	105·3	107·8
income data	101·7	99·9	100	103·4	105·3	108·0
output data	103·8	101·9	100	102·2	104·8	107·8
Average estimate	102·6	100·9	100	103·1	105·1	107·9

SOURCE
1979 *Blue Book*, Table 1.12. See also Tables 7.3 and 7.4 above.

7.5 Long Runs

Changes in real GDP are estimated from the constant-price valuation $\Sigma p_0 . q_t$, either directly for GDP(E) or under the disguise of a base-weighted average for GDP(O). Difficulties begin to arise as time goes on, and would usually become insurmountable when the base year has faded into the remote past, because of the increasingly rough approximations needed in matching current quantities with base prices. Most items change quite rapidly in brand, grade or quality and some items, such as fish-fingers or digital watches, in today's output have no relevant base price at all when the base is ten to twenty years ago.

Two questions arise. In the long run of twenty years or more, does it make any sense to ask how much higher the output or price level is now as compared with (e.g.) 1958 or 1938? In the shorter run of five years or so, even if $\Sigma p_0 . q_t$ *can* be estimated closely, *should* it be done? Relative prices do change over time. Real output is measured by values at *constant* prices but they should also be at *relevant* prices. It is quite possible, for example, to show changes in output in 1976–8 either at 1970 or at 1975 prices. It may be said, however, that the prices of 1970 have ceased to be relevant to what is produced in 1976–8 and that only constant 1975 prices are to be used.

Sooner or later, and generally sooner rather than later, the run of a quantity or price index needs to be stopped and replaced by a new index on a later base. The break in continuity which results needs to be bridged by linking together the old and the new runs. Over time, this process can be repeated on several occasions and it may even become possible to give sensible answers to the question of how much change there has been in outputs or prices between (e.g.) 1914 or 1938 and the present day.

When does a base need change? And how is a rebased index to be linked to the old one? These are practical questions with various answers. The well-known index of retail prices of the Department of Employment is of chain form with weights changed each January. Such a solution is not practicable for index numbers in the national accounts. It has become accepted, both here and abroad, that the best compromise is to rebase each five years starting with 1970 and to splice the new run on to the old run by a simple device: raise (or lower) the old run by a constant factor k so that it agrees with the new run in the year selected for splicing. The year s of the splicing is at choice; it may or may not be the new base year.

An index run of real output, spliced in this way, has most of the properties which are desirable. Up to year s, the run shows precisely the proportional changes from year to year of the old index and the comparisons are at relevant prices, those of the old base. From year s onwards, the new index takes over and comparisons are at the relevant prices of the new base – and it can be continued until the time comes to change base again. When the base of real GDP(E) and real GDP(O) was changed from 1970 to 1975, the splicing was done in 1973 in view of the large increase in oil prices at the end of that year. Relative prices in 1975 differed considerably from those in 1970. The splicing ensured that 1970 prices were appropriately used up to 1973 and 1975 prices thereafter.

There is, however, one awkward feature of the method of splicing adopted. It arises from the need to show real GDP both in total and analysed into various components. The method adopted is first to splice together the old and new runs for total GDP and then to do the same for each component separately. The raising factor k which brings the old index to the level of the new in the year of splicing differs from one component to another – and is different again for the total index. The consequence is that the values at constant prices of the real GDP index are such that components add to the total in any year from the year of splicing onwards, but not in earlier years.

Table 7.9 illustrates with real GDP(E) in 1972; the change is from constant prices in 1970 to those of 1975. The splicing is done in 1973, and the raising factors are in Column (3), varying from 1.2187 to 2.1711 for different components. The old run in 1972 based on 1970 is given in Column (4), components adding to total. To splice 1972 on to the new run based on 1975, the separate raising factors are applied and the Column (3) × (4) gives the components and the total in 1972 in the new run. The total is £88489 million at 1975 factor cost and the components add up to £88787 million, a difference of £298 million or 0·3 per cent. The difference tends to get rather larger for earlier years, as shown on p. 114 of the 1978 *Blue Book*.

The spliced run of the weighted-average index numbers for real GDP(O) has a similar lost property. In years from 1973, the components

TABLE 7.9 GDP(E): at 1970 and at 1975 factor cost (in £ million)

	1973 at 1970 factor cost (1)	1973 at 1975 factor cost (2)	Raising factor (2) – (1) (3)	1972 at 1970 factor cost (4)	1972 at 1975 factor cost (3) × (4)
Consumers' expenditure	36024	65497	1·8181	34521	62763
Government final consumption	10066	21426	2·1285	9608	20451
Gross domestic capital formation:					
Fixed	10294	21609	2·0992	9641	20238
Increase in stocks	1624	2983	1·8368	40	73
Exports of goods and services	14016	26147	1·8655	12486	23292
less imports of goods and services	−14298	−31043	2·1711	−12792	−27773
less adjustment to factor cost	−8971	−10933	1·2187	−8416	−10257
Real GDP(E)	48755	95686	1·9626	45088	88489

SOURCE
Based on 1978 *Blue Book*, Table 2.1.

combine into the total index by the use of the 1975 weights. Before 1973 the index numbers as raised by separate raising factors have components which cannot be combined into the total with either 1970 weights, or 1975 weights or any other fixed weights.

7.6 Effect of Base Changes

The introduction of a rebased index is a major operation and its first publication is some time – usually two or three years – after the year selected for the new base. The old index continues while the new one is in preparation. It is important to know what difference the new base is likely to make and to allow for it in advance.

The question can be examined in terms of a base-weighted index of output. In the usual algebraic notation, suppose the base is changed from year 0 to a later year 1 and write index numbers for changes from year s to a later year t (6.2 above):

Old index, base year 0: $\dfrac{\Sigma p_0 q_t}{\Sigma p_0 q_s} = \dfrac{1}{\Sigma w_0} \Sigma w_0 \dfrac{q_t}{q_s}$ $(w_0 = p_0 q_s)$

New index, base year 1: $\dfrac{\Sigma p_1 q_t}{\Sigma p_1 q_s} = \dfrac{1}{\Sigma w_1} \Sigma w_1 \dfrac{q_t}{q_s}$ $(w_1 = p_1 q_s)$

The difference arises from the application of different weights to the same quantity relative q_t/q_s. The weights w_0 and w_1 depend on relative prices – and not the level of prices – in base year 0 and in base year 1. The amount of the shift from the old to the new index is generally small since relative prices change slowly. It is large only when some significant changes have taken place in the price structure.

From the formulae above it can be seen that the direction of the shift depends on the correlation between the change from p_0 to p_1 (and so from w_0 to w_1) and the subsequent change from q_s to q_t. In the usual demand-dominated situation, the correlation is likely to be negative – large price increases between the base years tend to go with small increases in output subsequently. Hence it is to be expected that the new index, when introduced, shows a *lower* rate of growth than the old. It will go the other way only when there are enough items showing large price increases followed by large increases in output.

When real GDP(E) and real GDP(O) were rebased in 1978, the new runs on the 1975 base were carried back to the year of splicing (1973). A comparison of the old and new index numbers, therefore, can be made for the years from 1973 to 1977 inclusive. This is done in Table 7.10, taking the last 1970-based index numbers published (July 1978) and the first new ones on 1975 (September 1978).

TABLE 7.10 Real GDP: estimates before and after change to 1975 base

				% change	
	1973	*1975*	*1977*	*1973–5*	*1975–7*
GDP(E):					
at 1970 factor cost					
(£ millions)	48353	46811	48437	−3·2	+3·5
at 1975 factor cost					
(£ millions)	95686	92507	97119	−3·3	+5·0
GDP(O):					
1970–based (1970 = 100)	110·7	107·4	110·4	−3·0	+2·8
1975–based (1975 = 100)	103·8	100	104·8	−3·7	+4·8

SOURCE
Economic Trends (July 1978) and 1978 *Blue Book* (September 1978).

Output fell from 1973 to 1975, by a little over 3 per cent on the old index numbers and by about 3·5 per cent on the new. This small and downward shift is of the usual type. But for the growth from 1975 to 1977 the shift was unusual, both large and upwards. By early 1978, the 1970-based index numbers then published were showing a growth of about 3 per cent from 1975 to 1977. Shortly thereafter the 1975-based index numbers were published, showing a growth of nearly 5 per cent. Could this increase in the estimate have been anticipated? The answer is probably: yes. There were factors at work making for a positive correlation between price increases between 1970 and 1975 and rising output between 1975 and 1977. One factor was clear at the time: North Sea oil and gas. Oil prices increased sharply at the end of 1973 (between the two base years) and output from the North Sea fields expanded between 1975 and 1977.

The effect of this rebasing, both through revised weights and through the use of new or improved indicators, has been extensively explored in articles by the Central Statistical Office in *Economic Trends*. A background article by J. A. Rushbrook in No. 293, March 1978, was followed by three detailed articles, one again by Rushbrook and the others by J. V. Carter and D. C. K. Stirling, in No. 307, May 1979. They confirm that the main factor making for the upward revision of the growth rate in 1975–7 was indeed the oil price rise and the expansion of North Sea operations. The factor works directly on real GDP(O) through the mining component, but indirectly on real GDP(E) through the reduction of oil imports. There were, however, many other factors at work. In GDP(E) there was a significant effect of the more usual kind, partly offsetting the upward shift from reduced oil imports; real consumers' expenditure fell between 1973 and 1977, estimated at 3 per cent on the 1970-based index but at more than 4 per cent when 1975 is taken as the base year. Factors affecting the revision of real GDP(O) include such diverse ones as a large weight for potatoes in 1975 (a year of high prices), improved methods of deflating the value of construction work, and a change of indicator from numbers of telephone calls to minutes used.

It needs to be said in conclusion that a change of base year, even when it results in large revisions of the existing index numbers, is no cause for complaint. The index on the later base is a closer approximation to the changes being estimated and it should be introduced and used as soon as it can be made available.

8 Index Numbers of Price

8.1 Implied Price Index Numbers

Each Laspeyres index constructed to measure changes in output has a matching price index of implied (Paasche) form (7.2 above) and one of them was calculated and included in Table 7.3. There is a whole matrix of such price index numbers implied by GDP(E) at constant market prices and at constant factor cost, and by GDP(O) at constant factor cost, both in totals and for groups and sub-groups which make up the components.

The basic property, formula (B) of 6.3, is that a matching pair multiply to the value change and so separate the quantity and price movements. Once a quantity index in year t on year 0 as base is calculated, the implied price index follows without further computing from (C) of 6.3. In the usual notation:

$$\text{Implied prices index} = \frac{\Sigma p_t q_t}{\Sigma p_0 q_t} = \frac{V_{0t}}{Q_{0t}(p_0)} \tag{A}$$

Given the quantity measure as a constant price valuation ($\Sigma p_0 q_t$), the price index is got by dividing it into the current-price valuation of the same year ($\Sigma p_t q_t$). Table 7.1 and 7.2 are designed so that this can be done for expenditure aggregates. If it is the quantity index $Q_{0t}(p_0)$ which is given then it needs to be divided into the value change V_{0t}. Implied price index numbers come in this way from the totals and components of real GDP(O) in Table 7.4.

An implied price index is often described as a *deflator* since one of its uses is to deflate values to real terms. (A) can be rearranged as:

$$\text{Value at constant prices } (\Sigma p_0 q_t) = \frac{\text{Value at current prices } (\Sigma p_t q_t)}{\text{Implied price index}} \tag{B}$$

This is exact, by definition, when the denominator of (B) is the price index implied by the constant price valuation. But the deflation process

103

(B) can be applied, usefully if approximately, to a range of value aggregates by specifying the price index most nearly related to the aggregate. For example the consumers' expenditure deflator of Table 8.1 may be used to deflate total disposal income or a wages/salaries bill.

TABLE 8.1 Consumers' expenditure deflator

	1973	1974	1975	1976	1977	1978
Consumers' expenditure (in £ millions)						
at current market prices	45472	52088	63704	73765	84132	96086
at 1975 market prices	65911	64418	63704	63852	63313	66728
Deflator (1975 = 100)	69·0	80·9	100	115·5	132·9	144·0

SOURCE
Table 7.1, above.

One of the most used of the series of deflators on the expenditure side is the *consumers' expenditure deflator* calculated in Table 8.1. Similar deflators can be obtained for government final consumption, for gross domestic capital formation and, as pursued in 8.4 below, for exports or imports of goods and services. Deflators of wider scope are used in 8.3 below. At the end of the line, on reduction to factor cost, there is the *GDP deflator* implied by GDP (E) at constant factor cost and already given in Table 7.3 and used in Table 7.7.

The overall deflator on the output side, implied by GDP(O) at constant factor cost, is just another estimate of the GDP deflator. There are three measures of real GDP (Table 7.8 above) and each gives an estimate of the GDP deflator as its implied price index. Two are the same by the way real GDP(I) is defined (Table 7.7). There remain two alternative estimates of the single concept of the GDP deflator. Table 7.7B shows the GDP deflator from the expenditure side and the alternative estimate from the output side comes either by dividing the value change from Row (1) by the real GDP(O) index of Row (3) or equivalently by dividing values at current and constant factor cost from Rows (1) and (2).

The alternative estimates of the GDP deflator for 1973–8 are as set out in Table 8.2. The first is given explicitly in the 1979 *Blue Book* and it is the one used officially. The other can be calculated from the GDP(O) data in the *Blue Book* but it is not published as such. It provides a check on the first estimate.

The implied price index numbers which are published are given in

Table 2.5 of the *Blue Book*. They are wide in scope and all from the expenditure side. The GDP deflator at factor cost appears under its other title: *home costs per unit of output*. This serves to stress that the deflator is calculated by dividing GDP at current factor cost as home costs (including exports, excluding imports) by an index of real GDP representing the number of units of output.

TABLE 8.2 GDP deflator: alternative estimates (1975 = 100)

	1973	1974	1975	1976	1977	1978
Based on expenditure data	67·1	78·5	100	113·7	127·2	140·8
Based on output data	65·7	77·0	100	115·1	127·9	141·2

8.2 Published Price Data

It is worth making a brief digression to enquire why so few implied price index numbers are actually calculated and published in the national accounts. There are a few from the expenditure side and none from output data. Others are left to be calculated as needed by the user, from the annual data of the *Blue Book* and the seasonally adjusted quarterly series in *Economic Trends*.

This cannot be because a price index is less accurate than one of quantity. The quantity and price index numbers come from the same data with the same errors of estimation. If current values are closely estimated, then the basic property that matching index numbers multiply to the value change implies that errors in a quantity index appear as roughly equal and opposite errors in the price index. If the implied price index of Paasche form tends to understate price rises, it is because of Laspeyres quantity index overstates increases in output.

The reasons must be sought elsewhere. On the expenditure side, comprehensive figures on purchases of goods and services in real terms are not often available and the expenditure estimates at constant prices in the national accounts meet a genuine need – even though given only quarterly and annually after considerable delay. The position is different for prices. The systems of index numbers of wholesale and retail prices provide price data readily, quickly and frequently. An implied price index for (e.g.) furniture and floor coverings as a sub-group of consumers' expenditure can be calculated but it is neither as timely nor as accurate as the monthly index numbers calculated from price quotations for such items obtained direct from the shops.

The situation is even less favourable for price index numbers implied by estimates of GDP(O) at constant factor cost industry by industry. Real GDP(O) attempts to measure values added by industry in real terms and does so by using indicators of output or input (7.3 above). The method leads to great uncertainty on the meaning of the implied price index for an industry as the 'price' of value added. Certainly the system of monthly index numbers of wholesale prices is better for the job of deflating outputs and inputs.

8.3 Various Measures of Inflation

There are as many measures of inflation as there are views of what inflation is, and they are legion. It is assumed here that inflation relates to rising prices of goods and services produced or purchased by a specified group. A measure of inflation requires an answer to the question: inflation as experienced by what group and through what price rises?

The first measures sought are those applying to specific groups of consumers. The specification of the groups is a matter of choice. It may be the private sector of the national accounts: all residents together with unincorporated businesses and non-profitmaking bodies. The measure of inflation is then the consumers' expenditure deflator. Or it may be the narrower group taken by the Department of Employment in constructing their general retail prices index (RPI): all households except those getting most of their income from pensions and those where the head of household has an income above a specific cut-off point. Even narrower groups can be selected, as for the index numbers of retail prices for one-person and two-person pensioner households. See 'The Unstatistical Reader's Guide to the Retail Prices Index', *Department of Employment Gazette*, October 1975.

Other measures of inflation relate to the expenditure data of the national accounts and to the prices paid by all those involved in current transactions in money or as imputed. The precise coverage is conveniently seen in Figure 2.6 above.

Six measures of inflation are shown in Table 8.3. The first, the RPI, has the advantage that it is published monthly and rapidly; the others come from the quarterly and annual national accounts. A common way of showing inflation rates is as a percentage increase from one year to the

TABLE 8.3 Six measures of inflation (1975 = 100)

Price index numbers*	1973	1974	1975	1976	1977	1978
(1) Retail prices index (RPI)	69·4	80·5	100	116·5	135·0	146·2
Deflators for:						
(2) Consumers' expenditure	69·0	80·9	100	115·5	132·9	144·0
(3) Total domestic expenditure	66·8	80·1	100	115·0	130·5	142·5
(4) Total final expenditure	66·7	80·7	100	116·0	132·2	143·6
(5) GDP at market prices	68·4	78·6	100	114·4	130·1	143·4
(6) GDP at factor cost	67·1	78·5	100	113·7	127·2	140·8

NOTE
* All except Entry (6) at market prices. RPI of chained (Laspeyres) form, annual averages of monthly index, switched to 1975 as 100. Others are of implied (Paasche) form based on 1975.
SOURCE
Entry (1) from *Department of Employment Gazette*, Entry (2) from Table 8.1; the remainder are calculated from Table 7.2 above.

next. This is done in Table 8.4, where the six measures are grouped according to whether they do or do not include exports and imports.

TABLE 8.4 Annual rates of inflation, % increase from previous year

Inflation measure*	1974	1975	1976	1977	1978
With imports, not exports					
(1) RPI	16·0	24·2	16·5	15·9	8·3
(2) Consumers' expenditure	17·2	23·6	15·5	15·1	8·4
(3) Total domestic expenditure	19·9	24·8	15·0	13·5	9·2
With imports and exports					
(4) Total final expenditure	21·0	23·9	16·0	14·0	8·6
With exports, not imports					
(5) GDP at market prices	14·9	27·2	14·4	13·7	10·2
(6) GDP at factor cost	17·0	27·4	13·7	11·9	10·7

NOTE
All except Row (6) at market prices.
SOURCE
Table 8.3 above.

Entry (6) is a measure of pure domestic inflation. It represents home costs per unit of output (for sale at home or abroad), influenced neither by import prices nor by changes in rates of indirect taxes and subsidies. On this measure, the annual rate of inflation rose to nearly 28 per cent in 1975 and subsided to a little over 10 per cent in 1978.

Table 8.4 can then be read upwards to see the effect of changes in rates of indirect taxes and of prices of imports relative to those of exports. Net indirect taxes were important in 1976–7, when indirect tax rates were increased and subsidies reduced. Entry (5) shows higher inflation rates than (6) in these years. With imports added, Entry (4) shows higher rates in 1974 and 1976 because of large increases in import prices in those years. When the inflation measure is based on domestic expenditure as opposed to home costs, bringing in imports and leaving out exports, the relation of export to import prices, or the terms of trade (8.5 below), becomes a factor to consider. Favourable terms of trade, import prices rising more slowly, make for lower inflation rates and conversely. This is seen in the relative fluctuations of Entries (3) and (5), e.g. in the lower inflation rate of (3) when import prices rose less than export prices in 1978.

A comparison of Entries (1) and (2) with (3) shows how consumers fared under inflation as opposed to the economy as a whole. Consumers are much affected when net indirect taxes are raised. This is seen in 1976 and 1977 when net indirect taxes increased more than prices generally, pushing up the rate of inflation for consumers. The opposite was the case in 1974.

It can be concluded that the GDP deflator at factor cost stands up well; it is a measure of domestic inflation not directly affected by such external factors as import prices or by indirect taxes as changed in successive Budgets. But inflation is usually regarded as a movement in market prices paid by consumers, and index numbers such as the RPI or the consumers' expenditure deflator are at the mercy of variations in import prices and of changes in indirect taxes and subsidies. On the other hand they ignore income taxes. And yet there can be, and have been, major shifts between direct and indirect taxes. Should not these be taken into account in using an inflation measure based on market prices paid by consumers and, if so, how?

One way of dealing with this problem is to calculate real disposable income (9.3 below). The inflation measure used is the consumers' expenditure deflator, applied in reducing personal disposable income (after tax) to real terms. The result is a measure of the standard of living – real purchasing power after tax. A shift (e.g.) from direct to indirect taxes has its effect on real disposable income, an effect which can be in either direction. Lower income taxes increase disposable income while higher indirect taxes push up the inflation measure.

Such calculations, however, depend on the quarterly and annual national accounts. Something less leisurely may be needed: a monthly index to match the RPI but allowing for shifts between direct and indirect taxation. We have a clue: increases in *post-tax income* to maintain purchasing power are given by the RPI. Another index is needed, to measure increases in *gross income* which keep purchasing power constant. Such an index would be raised, like the RPI, by higher indirect taxation and it would be reduced by lower income taxes (more purchasing power in gross income) which leave the RPI unchanged.

The calculation of such an index – for gross income of constant purchasing power – is beset with practical difficulties. The index usually refers to an average earner and it is necessary to specify the gross income and tax allowances of each earner selected for the average. The calculations for each earner then proceed: deduct income tax from gross income in the base period; raise the resulting post-tax figure by multiplication by the inflation index used between the base and the current period; finally gross up at the current rates of income tax. This is only possible on the basis of a series of very specific and detailed assumptions. For example, does income include such transfers as child benefits; are National Insurance contributions deducted with income taxes; do the tax allowances used include those for dependents, for life assurance premiums, for mortgage payments and the like?

The Central Statistical Office calculates such an index: the monthly *tax and price index* (TPI), published in *Economic Trends*. It is of chain form with weights changed each January. It relates to an average tax unit – an individual or a married couple – as thrown up in the sample survey of personal income taxation made annually by the Inland Revenue. It excludes, in addition to those who pay no tax, those with gross earnings above a certain level. Hence the coverage of the TPI, though by no means identical with that of the retail prices index (RPI), is similar enough to set the two index numbers side by side. Details of the calculations – and of the assumptions made – are described in *Economic Trends*, No. 310, August 1979.

The RPI and TPI have specific uses, one measuring increases month by month in post-tax incomes, and the other gross incomes, to maintain purchasing power. A shift from indirect to direct taxation, as in 1974 and 1975, would raise the TPI more than the RPI; an opposite switch, as in 1979, would do the reverse.

An important application is to the problem of converting estimates of gross earnings to measures of real earnings. The Department of Employment publishes monthly index numbers of average earnings; they relate to gross earnings and no calculations are made of earnings after tax in money or in real terms. An approximate deflator of the earnings index for all employees is needed and the TPI is to be preferred to the RPI. This is why an index somewhat similar to the TPI and calculated by the Institute of Fiscal Studies is called the *gross earnings deflator* by the Institute.

TABLE 8.5 Average earnings (January 1978 = 100)

	1978		1979	
Index	*January*	*July*	*January*	*July*
RPI	100	104·5	109·3	120·9
TPI	100	100·5	106·1	113·8
Average earnings	100	110·0	111·7	128·0
Real average earnings*	100	109·4	105·3	112·5

* Deflation of average earnings by TPI.

Table 8.5 illustrates the data available in September 1979. The RPI is here switched from the base (January 1974) of the published index to January 1978 as 100. The index of average earnings is that for all employees (new series) and similarly switched from the base (January 1976) of the published series. No adjustments are made for seasonal variation.

8.4 Index Numbers for External Trade

Matching index numbers of volume and price for external trade in goods and services are obtained directly from Table 7.1. In view of the many uses of these index numbers, e.g. as measures of inflation in 8.3 above, it is worth while reviewing how the estimates are obtained and separating them into those for goods and those for services.

Statistics of trade in goods at current prices (5.2 above) come from the monthly returns published by the Department of Trade in *Overseas Trade Statistics* as adjusted to a balance of payments basis. The Department proceeds to calculate monthly index numbers of volume and price (unit value), both of Laspeyres form, following the method of the example in 6.5 above. The price index might be better calculated not as now from unit values, but from price quotations supplied by exporters and importers, so taking its place in the system of wholesale prices. This may become practicable in time.

Valuations in the national accounts of trade in goods at current and at constant (1975) prices are exactly those of the Department of Trade. The constant-price values are simply the Department's volume index numbers multiplied by trade in 1975. The only difference emerges when a price (unit value) index is written: a specially constructed index of Laspeyres form by the Department and an implied (Paasche) index, as usual, in the national accounts.

Trade in services at current prices (5.3 above) is estimated by the Central Statistical Office as a separate exercise for the national accounts and using a great variety of indicators. The corresponding estimates at constant (1975) prices follow without much extra difficulty by adjusting indicators to real terms, e.g. by deflation of values.

The results are current and constant-price series for exports and imports of goods and of services separately, and together as in Table 7.1 above. Index numbers of the volume of trade then follow from the values at constant (1975) prices by division by the 1975 value. They are set out in Table 8.6, those for goods being identical with the index numbers calculated by the Department of Trade. There are considerable

TABLE 8.6 External trade: volume index numbers* (1975 = 100)

	1973	1974	1975	1976	1977	1978
Exports:						
Goods	97·7	104·2	100	109·7	118·9	122·9
Services	92·2	98·1	100	107·4	111·2	109·8
Goods and services	96·2	102·5	100	109·1	116·7	119·1
Imports:						
Goods	108·8	109·7	100	105·6	107·2	112·6
Services	100·6	101·6	100	98·3	96·0	96·0
Goods and services	107·0	107·9	100	104·0	104·8	109·0

NOTE
* From values at constant (1975) prices.
SOURCE
1979 *Blue Book*, Table 2.1.

differences in the movement over time of real trade in goods and that in services. For example, exports of services in real terms fell off in 1978, and imports in 1976–7, during years when trade in goods continued to grow in real terms.

Table 8.7 assembles the index numbers of price (unit value), both those for goods calculated by the Department of Trade in Laspeyres

TABLE 8.7 External trade: price (Unit Value) index numbers* (1975 = 100)

	1973	1974	1975	1976	1977	1978
Department of Trade index:						
Exports: Goods	64·1	81·7	100	120·7	142·5	155·1
Imports: Goods	59·6	87·4	100	121·8	141·3	146·4
Blue Book index:						
Exports: Goods	63·7	81·5	100	119·0	139·0	148·2
Services	73·2	87·2	100	121·4	135·6	144·8
Goods and Services	66·3	83·0	100	119·7	138·1	147·3
Imports: Goods	58·7	87·4	100	121·0	139·2	143·2
Services	70·4	87·6	100	125·0	141·7	146·9
Goods and Services	61·1	87·5	100	121·8	139·7	143·9

NOTE
* *Department of Trade* index, annual averages of monthly index of Laspeyres form; *Blue Book* index of implied (Paasche) form.
SOURCE
Economic Trends and 1979 *Blue Book*, Tables 1.7 and 2.1.

form and those for goods and services in the implied (Paasche) form of the national accounts. The prices of services entering into external trade rose more slowly than for goods during 1973–5. The movements after 1975 were less divergent.

8.5 The Terms of Trade and the Trade Gain

These two constructs arise in an attempt to quantify how favourable to this country is the external trading in goods and services. They are conveniently defined in terms of a simple algebraic notation. Write P_x, Q_x and $V_x = P_x Q_x$ for price, volume and current value of exports and P_m for import prices. As a concept, the *terms of trade* may be defined:

$$\text{Terms of trade: } T = \frac{\text{Receipts from one unit of exports}}{\text{Price of imports}} = \frac{P_x}{P_m} \quad \text{(A)}$$

This says nothing at all about what trade actually takes place. T shows the volume of imports which can be got from one unit of exports solely on the basis of relative prices. The price of exports can rise relative to imports – a change regarded as favourable – and the volume of exports can fall off if they price themselves out of their market.

In practice, T cannot be measured by the ratio of export to import prices as suggested by (A). Prices are not additive; P_x and P_m are index numbers on a base year and so is T. Hence the practical interpretation of (A) is not the level of the terms of trade but changes in the terms over time. So T is the ratio of an index of export prices to an index of import prices and it is measured from the base of the index numbers used. In particular, the terms of trade are said to improve or to become favourable if T increases: i.e. if export prices rise faster than import prices.

T can be calculated for all external trade or for any sector. It is shown in Table 8.8 for goods and services separately and together. The index of the Department of Trade for goods is available monthly and quickly. Only the *Blue Book* index is available, quarterly and annually, for the wider terms of trade in goods and services.

TABLE 8.8 Terms of trade* (1975 = 100)

	1973	1974	1975	1976	1977	1978
Department of Trade: Goods	107·6	93·5	100	99·1	100·8	105·9
Blue Book: Goods	108·5	93·2	100	98·3	99·9	103·5
Services	104·0	99·5	100	97·1	95·7	98·6
Goods and Services	108·5	94·9	100	98·3	98·9	102·4

NOTE
* Ratio of export to import price index numbers.
SOURCE
Table 8.7, above.

Suppose the terms of trade improve without exports falling off in volume. It would seem to follow not only that there is a gain from external trade – otherwise there would be no trade – but also that the gain is increasing. This needs to be quantified. Several measures of the gain from trade have been suggested, as conveniently summarised in J. Hibbert, 'Measuring Changes in the Nation's Real Income', *Economic Trends*, No. 255, January 1975. The most frequently used measure is also the simplest: the excess of the volume of imports which can be purchased from the proceeds of actual exports over the volume of these exports:

$$\text{Trade gain: } G = \frac{\text{Value of exports}}{\text{Price of imports}} - \frac{\text{Value of exports}}{\text{Price of exports}}$$

$$= V_x \left(\frac{1}{P_m} - \frac{1}{P_x} \right) \tag{B}$$

If the actual volume of exports is given, G measures what imports by volume can be obtained. If G rises, there is an increase in the gain from trade in the sense that a given volume of exports can be traded for a higher volume of imports.

In practice, P_x and P_m are index numbers on a base year and G measures not the absolute gain from trade, but the increase from the base year. To check: for the base year, $P_x = P_m = 1$ and $G = 0$. Further, each of the terms of (B) is a deflated value, in £million at the constant prices of the base year. If $G > 0$, the trade gain has grown since the base year. If $G < 0$, there is a loss – but no indication to stop trading. The trade gain is simply lower in the current than in the base year.

It now follows that there are two factors at work. From (A) and (B)

$$G = P_x Q_x \left(\frac{1}{P_m} - \frac{1}{P_x} \right) = Q_x \left(T - 1 \right)$$

and the trade gain varies directly with the excess of T over its base value (unity) and with the volume of exports. This is illustrated by Table 8.9, which calculates the gain from trade in goods and services in 1976–8 over the base year 1975. In this period the terms of trade fell sharply in 1976 and then recovered (Table 8.8). As some offset, the volume of exports increased (Q_x in Table 8.9). Even so, the trade gain fell by a moderate amount of about £500 million at 1975 prices from 1975 to 1976, recovered a little in 1977 and rose above the 1975 level only in 1978.

TABLE 8.9 External trade in goods and services: trade gain

		1975	1976	1977	1978
Value of exports (in £ million):					
at current prices	V_x	27145	35435	43735	47636
at 1975 prices	Q_x	27145	29611	31679	32343
Price (unit value) index (1975 = 100):					
Exports	$100P_x$	100	119·7	138·1	147·3
Imports	$100P_m$	100	121·8	139·7	143·9
Trade gain from 1975 (in £ million):					
at 1975 prices $\quad G = V_x \left(\dfrac{1}{P_m} - \dfrac{1}{P_x} \right)$		—	− 510	− 362	+ 764

SOURCE
Tables 7.1 and 8.7, above.

9 Real Disposable Income and Expenditure

9.1 Introduction

It is now time to take up the loose strand left at the beginning of 2.4 above. At current market prices, gross national income is identically equal both to gross national product as the value of the goods and services *produced* and to gross national expenditure as the value of the different set of goods and services *purchased* out of income. This identity ceases to hold on deflation to real terms.

One constituent of real GNP is the volume of exports, V_x/P_x in the notation of 8.5 above. Gross national expenditure includes the purchase not of the exports, but of the imports for which they are traded. The corresponding real constituent is the volume of imports obtainable from exports, V_x/P_m in the present notation. Hence real gross national expenditure is different from real GNP and exceeds it by V_x/P_m *less* V_x/P_n which is the trade gain G.

This makes sense. The real expenditure of UK nationals out of income is their standard of living. In the absence of external trade, they can only purchase what they produce. With external trade they can do better. Because of the trade gain, they raise their living standard without working harder. In practice, the trade gain G and so the excess of real expenditure over real product are calculated from index numbers on a given base year. What is measured is the increase (+) or decrease(−) in the trade gain from the base year and so the corresponding change in the excess of real expenditure over real product.

9.2 Real Consumers' Expenditure

Real expenditure can be viewed first from the angle of the personal sector, in terms of expenditure out of personal disposable income (Table 4.2, above). The main aggregate here is consumers' expenditure.

The usual index numbers can be used to split a change in consumers' expenditure into the part arising from price movements and the part which is a volume change. The level of prices affecting a group of consumers can be called their *cost of living* and their real consumption is their *standard of living*. These complementary concepts are measured in practice in their changes over time by means of index numbers.

The term 'cost of living' has often been used somewhat loosely. The present meaning is clear enough: the cost of purchasing a fixed 'basket' of goods and services deemed appropriate to the consumers considered. This is what is done in the first two measures of inflation of Table 8.3. They should be linked with a corresponding measure of the changing standard of living of the same consumers.

The retail price index (RPI) measures the changing cost month by month of a 'basket' of commodities fixed in the base period as the average purchases of the group of families covered by the index. Since the index is chained, the 'basket' is adjusted each January and then remains fixed over the following twelve months. There is no precise index published to represent the volume of consumption of the group of families. The index of retail sales, published monthly in real terms, has a less wide coverage of goods and services.

The second inflation measure of Table 8.3 is the consumers' expenditure deflator for the whole group of consumers in the national accounts. As a Paasche form it shows the changing cost of a fixed 'basket' of commodities, that of the current year. It is matched by a Laspeyres volume index showing changes in real consumers' expenditure. Table 8.1 gives both the consumers' expenditure deflator and the consumers' expenditure at constant (1975) prices. Table 9.1 reproduces them and also shows, by division through by the 1975 value, the volume index with 1975 as 100.

The consumers' expenditure deflator serves as an index of the cost of living of the whole group of consumers. The index of real consumers' expenditure is not quite the corresponding measure of the standard of living. It is dependent, as the price index is not, on the size of the group. However, a standard of living index can be arrived at by taking real consumers' expenditure per head of the population. The adjustment is small since population changes slowly. Between 1975 and 1978, for example, the cost of living increased by about 45 per cent and the standard of living by only 4·8 per cent on adjusting real consumers' expenditure for a small population decline of 0·1 per cent.

Two points are to be noticed. First, real consumers' expenditure per head is an average of arithmetic form and, as such, influenced more by

TABLE 9.1 Real personal disposable income

	1973	1974	1975	1976	1977	1978
At current market prices:						
Consumers' expenditure (in £ millions)	45472	52088	63704	63765	84132	96086
Personal disposable income (in £ millions)	51100	60686	74707	86382	97748	113300
Percentage saving*	11·0	14·2	14·7	14·6	13·9	15·2
Consumers' expenditure deflator (1975 = 100)	69·0	80·9	100	115·5	132·9	144·0
At 1975 market prices:						
Consumers' expenditure (in £ millions)	65911	64418	63704	63852	63313	66728
1975 = 100	103·5	101·1	100	100·2	99·4	104·7
Personal disposable income (in £ millions)	74069	75051	74707	74773	73560	78682
1975 = 100	99·1	100·5	100	100·1	98·5	105·3

NOTE
* Balance of personal disposable income over consumers' expenditure as percentage of personal disposable income.

SOURCE
1979 *Blue Book*, Table 4.1. See also Tables 4.1, 4.2 and 8.1 above.

those with high than with low expenditures. Then the standard of living measured is that achieved on average by consumers out of their take-home pay. It ignores benefits from social security schemes, from the provision of defence and from other services supplied by government out of taxation and National Insurance funds.

9.3 Real Personal Disposable Income

Real consumers' expenditure has one limitation as a measure of standards of living. It depends on how consumers choose to divide their disposable income between consumption and saving, a choice influenced by a variety of factors operating in the short and in the long run. It is better, for many purposes, to use personal disposable income in real terms instead.

Personal disposable income, as total personal income *less* taxes on income, National Insurance contributions and net transfers to abroad, divides into consumers' expenditure and saving (Table 4.2 above). Consumers regard personal disposable income as available for spending and saving as postponed consumption. Real personal disposable income is appropriately obtained by deflation, like consumers' expenditure, by the consumers' expenditure deflator. This is shown in Table 9.1 both as a value at constant (1975) prices and as an index with 1975 as 100. As a measure of purchasing power or standard of living, on average over all consumers, the index of real personal disposable income needs a small adjustment for population change (a fall of between 0·1 and 0·2 per cent from 1973 to 1978).

On this measure, the consumers' standard of living remained almost constant from 1973 to 1976, fell away in 1977 and recovered in 1978. The fact that consumers actually consumed less in real terms between 1973 and 1975 is a reflection of the change in saving as boom turned into recession. Saving as a percentage of personal disposable income, already high in 1973, increased sharply in 1974.

9.4 Gross National Disposable Income (GNDI)

Gross national income as earned is the sum of GDP and net property income from abroad, an aggregate from which transfers of all kinds are excluded. Hence, when spending is considered, transfers to abroad (net of those from abroad) need to be met out of income. By formula (G) of

2.2 above, gross national income is spent as gross national expenditure, the sum of total domestic expenditure on consumption and investment, net transfers to abroad and net investment abroad.

A variant is appropriate to the present consideration of disposable income: gross national income *less* net transfers to abroad. This is called *gross national disposable income*, GNDI for short. It can be shown in two ways at current prices:

GNDI as earned = GDP *plus* net property income from $\Big\}$ **(A)**
    abroad *less* net transfers to abroad

GNDI as spent = total domestic expenditure $\Big\}$ **(B)**
    plus net investment abroad

It is an extension of personal disposable income – which goes on consumption at home and the provision of funds for investment in the form of personal saving – from the personal sector to the whole economy on the national level.

By definition, (A) and (B) are identical totals at current prices. Table 9.2 shows (A) in the top half and (B) in the bottom half from 1975 to 1978. Here GDP like total domestic expenditure is estimated from the expenditure side so that (A) and (B) are consistent. The adjusting items are all net figures which can take either sign. For this country it happens that net property income from abroad and net transfers to abroad are almost inevitably positive. The sign of net investment abroad oscillates between positive in good and negative in bad years.

TABLE 9.2 Gross national disposable income (GNDI) (in £ millions at market prices)

	1975	1976	1977	1978
Gross domestic product	103949	123348	142128	161639
plus net property income from abroad	+762	+1299	+201	+836
less net transfers to abroad	−510	−797	−1155	−1918
GNDI	104201	123850	141174	160557
Total domestic expenditure	105822	124692	140881	159525
plus net investment abroad	−1621	−842	+293	+1032

SOURCE
1979 *Blue Book*, Tables 1.1 and 1.7.

9.5 Real GNDI

It remains to express GNDI as expenditure in real terms and, in relating it to real product, to show up the effect of the trade gain. The notation of 8.5 is again used and NPI is written for net property income from abroad *less* net transfers to abroad. Market prices are used throughout.

Real GNDI as expenditure is the deflation of (B) of 9.4 above. The first term becomes total domestic expenditure at constant prices. Net investment abroad is the balance of trade in goods and services, of property income and of transfers to and from abroad. At current prices:

$$\text{Net investment abroad} = V_x - V_m + \text{NPI}$$

Since investment abroad is to be regarded as postponed imports, the appropriate deflator is the price index P_m of imports of goods and services:

$$\frac{V_x - V_m + \text{NPI}}{P_m} = \frac{V_x}{P_x} - \frac{V_m}{P_m} + V_x \left(\frac{1}{P_m} - \frac{1}{P_x} \right) + \frac{\text{NPI}}{P_m}$$

The penultimate term here is the trade gain G (8.5 above). So:

$$\text{Real GNDI as spent} = \text{total domestic expenditure at constant prices}$$
$$+ \frac{V_x}{P_x} - \frac{V_m}{P_m} + G + \frac{\text{NPI}}{P_m}$$
$$= \text{real GDP} + G + \frac{\text{NPI}}{P_m}$$

The calculation of real GNDI on this formula is shown in Table 9.3.

The appearance of G here is as expected (9.1 above). To check: (A) of 9.4 above gives GNDI as earned from production as (GDP + NPI) at current prices and as (real GDP + NPI/P_m) in real terms. This differs from real GNDI as expenditure by the trade gain G.

Table 9.3 shows both real GDP and real GNDI as expenditure in index form with 1975 as 100. These two index series are calculated (and published) in the *Blue Book* with two refinements not made in Table 9.3. One is that real GDP is taken as the average of estimates from expenditure, income and output data and not from the expenditure side alone. The other is that allowance is made for the way in which import duties are included in practice in GDP at market prices. See J. Hibbert,

TABLE 9.3 Real GNDI

		1975	1976	1977	1978
At 1975 market prices (in £ millions):					
Gross domestic product	(1)	103949	107815	109259	112682
plus adjustment for trade gain	(2)	–	−510	−362	+764
plus net property income from abroad	(3)	+762	+1066	+144	+581
less net transfers to abroad	(4)	−510	−654	−827	−1333
Real GNDI		104201	107717	108214	112694
Index numbers, 1975 = 100:					
Real GDP at market prices		100	103·7	105·1	108·4
Real GNDI at market prices		100	103·4	103·9	108·2

SOURCE
Rows (1) from Table 7.2, (2) from Table 8.9, (3) and (4) from Table 9.2 on deflation by price index for imports of goods and services from Table 8.7 above.

'Measuring Changes in the Nation's Real Income,' *Economic Trends*, No. 255, January 1975. As Table 9.4 shows, the differences are not large as compared with the unadjusted series of Table 9.3 above.

TABLE 9.4 Real GDP and real GNDI at market prices (1975 = 100)

	1975	1976	1977	1978
Real GDP at market prices	100	103·2	105·0	108·5
Real GNDI at market prices	100	103·0	104·0	108·6

SOURCE
1979 *Blue Book*, Table 1.12

In real GNDI we have the widest measure of the standard of living of UK nationals. It is wider in scope than real earnings (8.3, above) or real personal disposable income (9.3, above). It is obtained, as set out in Table 9.3, by two adjustments to real GDP at market prices, representing what is produced within the domestic economy. First, real property income from abroad is brought in, measured net and adjusted for net transfers to abroad. This turns a domestic into a national concept. Then, to get the national standard of living – to see what expenditures can be achieved from the product – allowance is made for changes in the trade gain.

The product of the domestic economy increased fairly steadily in the years of recovery from 1975 to 1978. The national standard of living increased more slowly in 1976 because of a reduced trade gain, and again in 1977 because of a fall in real property income from abroad. There was then a marked recovery in living standards in 1978. We have seen (Table 9.1 above) that real personal disposable income rose by 7·0 per cent in 1978, but this was following a fall in 1977. The wider measure of real GNDI is less erratic: a small increase of 1 per cent in 1977 and a larger one of 4·4 per cent in 1978. This compares with the rise in real GDP at market prices of only 3·3 per cent in 1978.

Index